Lecture Notes in Computer Science

T0253832

Commenced Publication in 1973
Founding and Former Series Editors:
Gerhard Goos, Juris Hartmanis, and Jan van Leeuwen

Hyun Soo Park   Albert Ali Salah
Yong Jae Lee   Louis-Philippe Morency
Yaser Sheikh   Rita Cucchiara (Eds.)

Human Behavior Understanding

5th International Workshop, HBU 2014
Zurich, Switzerland, September 12, 2014
Proceedings

 Springer

Volume Editors

Hyun Soo Park
University of Pennsylvania
Philadelphia, PA, USA
E-mail: hypar@seas.upenn.edu

Yong Jae Lee
University of California
Davis, CA, USA
E-mail: yjlee22@eecs.berkeley.edu

Yaser Sheikh
Carnegie Mellon University
Robotics Institute
Pittsburgh, PA, USA
E-mail: yaser@cs.cmu.edu

Albert Ali Salah
Boğaziçi University
Dept. of Computer Engineering
Istanbul, Turkey
E-mail: salah@boun.edu.tr

Louis-Philippe Morency
University of Southern California
Playa Vista, CA, USA
E-mail: morency@ict.usc.edu

Rita Cucchiara
Università degli Studi di Modena e
Reggio Emilia, Dip. di Ingegneria
"Enzo Ferrari" (DIEF)
Modena, Italy
E-mail: cucchiara.rita@unimore.it

ISSN 0302-9743
ISBN 978-3-319-11838-3
DOI 10.1007/978-3-319-11839-0
Springer Cham Heidelberg New York Dordrecht London

e-ISSN 1611-3349
e-ISBN 978-3-319-11839-0

Library of Congress Control Number: 2014949197

LNCS Sublibrary: SL 6 – Image Processing, Computer Vision, Pattern Recognition, and Graphics

Typesetting: Camera-ready by author, data conversion by Scientific Publishing Services, Chennai, India

Printed on acid-free paper

Springer is part of Springer Science+Business Media (www.springer.com)

Preface

Domains where human behavior understanding is a crucial need (e.g., robotics, human-computer interaction, affective computing, and social signal processing) rely on advanced pattern recognition techniques to automatically interpret complex behavioral patterns generated when humans interact with machines or with others. This is a challenging problem where many issues are still open, including the joint modeling of behavioral cues taking place at different time scales, the inherent uncertainty of machine detectable evidences of human behavior, the mutual influence of people involved in interactions, the presence of long term dependencies in observations extracted from human behavior, and the important role of dynamics in human behavior understanding.

The Fifth Workshop on Human Behavior Understanding (HBU), organized as a satellite to the European Conference on Computer Vision (ECCV 2014, Zürich), gathered researchers dealing with the problem of modeling human behavior under its multiple facets (expression of emotions, display of relational attitudes, performance of individual or joint actions, imitation, etc.). The HBU Workshops, previously organized jointly with Int. Conf. on Pattern Recognition (ICPR 2010, Istanbul), Int. Joint Conf. on Ambient Intelligence (AMI 2011, Amsterdam) IEEE/RSJ Int. Conf. on Intelligent Robots and Systems (IROS 2012, Algarve), and ACM Multimedia (ACM MM 2013, Barcelona), highlight different aspects of this problem since its inception.

The 5th HBU Workshop focused on **computer vision for complex social interactions**. Vision is a major modality for detecting social signals, analysis of facial and bodily affect, motion of interacting people in dyads or crowds. Following ECCV traditions, the Workshop featured eight invited talks by active researchers and leaders of the field.

The first invited talk, by Dr. Fei-Fei Li (Stanford University), focused on her recent work in large-scale crowd forecasting. She proposed to quantitatively study crowded environments by introducing a dataset of 42 million trajectories collected in train stations. Based on this dataset, she has shown a method to predict pedestrians behaviors. She introduced a new descriptor coined as Social Affinity Map (SAM) to link broken or unobserved trajectories of individuals in the crowd, while using the origin and destination priors. Her experiments show that improvements in performance can be gained through the use of SAM features.

The second invited talk was by Dr. Marco Cristani (University of Verona), entitled "From Groups to Crowds: a Social Signal Processing Perspective". In his talk, Dr. Cristani built on concepts inherited from sociological analysis and offered a detailed taxonomy of groups and crowds. This analysis individuates many typologies of social gatherings, each with its own characteristics and behavior dynamics. These differences are not only useful for a mere classification purpose, but are crucial when the need of automatic modeling comes into play, selecting particular computer vision techniques and models as the most appropriate to account for such differences. In particular, Dr. Cristani focused on a specific kind of group, i.e. free-standing conversational group, and one kind of crowd, i.e. spectator crowd, showing recent advances in their automatic modeling.

The third invited talk by Dr. David Forsyth (University of Illinois at Urbana-Champaign) dealt with human activity understanding. He presented a short overview of the state-of-the-art computer vision techniques, such as structure from motion, detection, classification, and tracking, illustrating how computational activity understanding can leverage these techniques. Through his talk, he tackled the following fundamental questions of human activity understanding: "What are they doing?"; "Where are they doing it?"; "Why are they doing it?"; "What will happen?" He argued that these techniques are not yet reliable enough to be directly applicable to challenging behavior understanding studies and illustrated the open problems of computational representations and semantics.

The next invited talk was by Dr. Jim Rehg (Georgia Institute of Technology), entitled "Social Interactions from an Egocentric Perspective". Dr. Rehg presented his recent work in egocentric analysis of social interactions, with a particular focus on the automatic analysis of children's social behaviors. He showed results in analyzing group social interactions and detecting bids for eye contact by a child during interactions with an adult clinician. He also outlined the potential for these methods to impact the identification and treatment of developmental disorders such as autism.

The fifth invited talk by Dr. Nicu Sebe (University of Trento) was entitled "Human Behavior Understanding in the Wild". Dr. Sebe discussed several related problems that fit into this current trend of human behavior analysis. He presented his recent research on head pose estimation from low-resolution, monocular and multi-view surveillance data. While the state-of-the-art approaches still work poorly under target motion, as facial appearance is distorted by camera perspective and scale changes when a person moves around, Dr. Sebe and colleagues have developed a novel framework based on Multi-Task Learning for classifying the head pose of a person, who moves freely in an environment monitored by multiple, large field-of-view surveillance cameras. Finally, he discussed the problems of facial expression recognition under extreme head poses and about constructing person specific models for facial expression recognition.

The sixth invited talk by Dr. Shai Avidan (Tel-Aviv University) was on the photo-sequencing framework, which exploits socially captured images. Dynamic events such as family gatherings, concerts or sports events are often captured by a group of people. The set of still images obtained this way is rich in dynamic content, but lacks accurate temporal information. Dr. Avidan addressed the problem of temporal synchronization of multiple cameras for a dynamic scene. His research explores geometric relationships between images and uses rank aggregation to find a global order of images.

The seventh invited talk was by Dr. Daniel Gatica-Perez (Idiap Research Institute), which dealt with the analysis of conversational vlogs. This is a novel approach to the study of personality impressions in social media, using crowd-sourced impressions, social attention, and audiovisual behavioral analysis on slices of conversational vlogs extracted from YouTube. Dr. Gatica-Perez showed that research in vlogs may become a fertile ground for the study of video interactions, as conversational video expands to innovative applications. In their research, his group addressed the task of automatic prediction of vloggers' personality impressions using nonverbal cues and machine learning techniques.

The final invited talk by Dr. Alessandro Vinciarelli (University of Glascow) was entitled "Social Signal Processing: Understanding Nonverbal Behavior in Social Interactions". Social signal processing is the domain aimed at modeling, analysis and synthesis of nonverbal behavior in social interactions. The core idea of the field is that nonverbal cues, the wide spectrum of nonverbal behaviors accompanying human-human and human-machine interactions (facial expressions, vocalizations, gestures, postures, etc.), are the physical, machine detectable evidence of social and psychological phenomena not otherwise accessible to observation. Analyzing conversations in terms of nonverbal behavioral cues, whether this means turn-organization, prosody or voice quality, allows one to automatically detect and understand phenomena like conflict, roles, personality, quality of rapport, etc.

This proceedings volume contains the papers presented at the workshop. We received 18 submissions in total, and each paper was peer-reviewed by at least two members of the Technical Program Committee. Four papers were accepted as oral presentations, and five papers were presented as posters. The papers are organized into thematic sections on Social Signals, Face and Affect, Motion Analysis, and Multiparty Interactions. Together with the invited talks, the focus theme was covered broadly and extensively by the workshop.

We would like to take the opportunity to thank our Program Committee members and reviewers for their rigorous feedback, our authors and our invited speakers for their contributions.

September 2014

Hyun Soo Park
Albert Ali Salah
Yong Jae Lee
Louis-Philippe Morency
Yaser Sheikh
Rita Cucchiara

Organization

Conference Co-chairs

Hyun Soo Park   University of Pennsylvania, USA
Albert Ali Salah   Boğaziçi University, Turkey
Yong Jae Lee   University of California, Davis, USA
Louis-Philippe Morency   University of Southern California, USA
Yaser Sheikh   Carnegie Mellon University, USA
Rita Cucchiara   University of Modena and Reggio Emilia, Italy

Technical Program Committee

Hamid Aghajan   Stanford University, USA
Oya Aran   Idiap Research Institute, Switzerland
Richard Bowden   University of Surrey, UK
Wongun Choi   NEC Laboratories America, USA
Peter Carr   Disney Research, USA
Marco Cristani   University of Verona, Italy
Fernando de la Torre   Carnegie Mellon University, USA
Laurence Devillers   LIMSI, France
Hamdi Dibeklioğlu   Delft University of Technology,
        The Netherlands
Pnar Duygulu Sahin   Bilkent University, Turkey
Hazm Ekenel   Istanbul Technical University, Turkey
Alireza Fathi   Stanford University, USA
Raquel Fernandez Rovira   University of Amsterdam, The Netherlands
Roland Goecke   University of Canberra, Australia
Jordi Gonzalez   UAB-CVC Barcelona, Spain
Hatice Gunes   Queen Mary University of London, UK
Alexander Hauptmann   Carnegie Mellon University, USA
Hayley Hung   Delft University of Technology,
        The Netherlands
Nazli Ikizler-Cinbis   Hacettepe University, Turkey
Quiang Ji   Ransellaer Polytechnic Institute, USA
Mohan Kankanhalli   National University of Singapore, Singapore
Cem Keskin   Microsoft Research, UK
Kris Kitani   Carnegie Mellon University, USA
Ivan Laptev   Inria, France
Patrick Lucey   Disney Research, USA

Simon Lucey	Carnegie Mellon University, USA
Jean Marc Odobez	Idiap Research Institute, Switzerland
Greg Mori	Simon Fraser University, Canada
Vittorio Murino	Istituto Italiano di Tecnologia and University of Verona, Italy
Massimo Piccardi	University of Technology, Australia
Michael Ryoo	NASA Jet Propulsion Laboratory, USA
Shishir Shah	University of Houston, USA
Alan Smeaton	Dublin City University, Ireland
Leonid Sigal	Disney Research, USA
Khiet Truong	University of Twente, The Netherlands

Additional Reviewers

Wen-Sheng Chu
Rajitha Navarathna

Table of Contents

How Do You Like Your Virtual Agent?: Human-Agent Interaction Experience through Nonverbal Features and Personality Traits

Aleksandra Cerekovic[1,2], Oya Aran[1], and Daniel Gatica-Perez[1,3]

[1] Idiap Research Institute, Martigny, Switzerland
[2] University of Zagreb, Faculty of Electrical Engineering and Computing, Zagreb, Croatia
[3] Ecole Polytechnique Federal de Lausanne (EPFL), Lausanne, Switzerland

Abstract. Recent studies suggest that human interaction experience with virtual agents can be, to a very large degree, described by people's personality traits. Moreover, the nonverbal behavior of a person has been known to indicate several social constructs in different settings. In this study, we analyze human-agent interaction from the perspective of the personality of the human and the nonverbal behaviors he/she displays during the interaction. Based on existing work in psychology, we designed and recorded an experiment on human-agent interactions, in which a human communicates with two different virtual agents. Human-agent interactions are described with three self-reported measures: quality, rapport and likeness of the agent. We investigate the use of self-reported personality traits and extracted audio-visual nonverbal features as descriptors of these measures. Our results on a correlation analysis show significant correlations between the interaction measures and several of the personality traits and nonverbal features, which are supported by both psychology and human-agent interaction literature. We further use traits and nonverbal cues as features to build regression models for predicting measures of interaction experience. Our results show that the best results are obtained when nonverbal cues and personality traits are used together.

Keywords: human-agent interaction, quality of interaction, nonverbal behavior, Big 5 personality traits.

1 Introduction

A growing number of applications seek to provide social abilities and human-like intelligence to computers. Compelling social interactions with computers, or specifically Embodied Conversational Agents (ECAs), are persuasive, engaging, and they increase trust and feeling of likeness, so it is understandable why recent trends show increasing usage of virtual agents in social media, education or social coaching.

Clearly, with the advance of social, user-aware adaptive interfaces, it has become increasingly important to model and reason social judgment for agents.

H.S. Park et al. (Eds.): HBU 2014, LNCS 8749, pp. 1–15, 2014.
© Springer International Publishing Switzerland 2014

To help virtual agents to interpret the human behaviors a number of observation studies has been proposed: human conversational behaviors are induced in (mainly, with the Wizard-of-Oz) experiments with agents, or in interaction with other humans. Further, observed behaviors are used to model both perception and reasoning components for the agents.

Several studies investigated the impact of human personality on the outcomes of human-agent interaction (HAI) and on the evaluation of the agent, with a goal to understand human preference for interactive characters. In most of those works, only the extraversion trait has been considered as the personality trait to analyze. The most notable studies on this topic come from the early 2000s. Limited by technology, researchers used only vocal behaviors [19], or a still image and textual interfaces [10] to simulate the extraverted/intraverted agent. In similar and more recent studies extraversion is manipulated via computer-generated voice and gestures of 2D cartoon-like agent [5]. As outcomes, it has been shown how humans are attracted by characters who have both similar personality, confirming similarity rule, and opposite personality, confirming complementary rule (see [5] for an overview).

Other recent studies have started to observe influence of personality traits other than extraversion to various social phenomena of HAI, such as rapport, or perception of agent's personality [17]. In [28], two conditions (low and high behaviour realism) of an agent designed to build rapport (the Rapport agent) were manipulated in interaction with humans. Further, human personality traits were correlated with persistent behavioral patterns, such as shyness or fear of interpersonal encounters. The results of the study have shown how both extraversion and agreeableness have been recognized to have a major impact on human attitudes, more than gender and age. Other Big 5 traits, namely neuroticism, openness to experience and consciousness were not found significant. Another study with the Rapport agent compared the perceived rapport of HAI to the rapport experienced in human-human conversation [12]. Results indicate how people who score higher in agreeableness perceived strong rapport both with the agent and a human, with a stronger relationship for the agent than human. Moreover, people with higher conscientiousness reported strong rapport when they communicated with both the agent and a human. A first-impression study [6] analyzed the impact of human personality on human judgments of the agents across conditions in which agents displayed different nonverbal behaviors (proximity and amount of smiles and gazing). Judgments included agent's extraversion and friendliness. The study has shown how agent smiles had a main effect on judging of friendliness, showing positive correlation between smiles and friendliness. However, the relation between human personality and perceived interaction in this study is not that evident: it has only been concluded that people with low agreeableness tend to interpret agents who gaze more as friendlier.

In this paper, we build an experimental study to investigate the influence of human personality to perceived experience of HAI. We also study how humans' audio-visual nonverbal cues can be used to reveal perceived experience. We further experiment with regression models to predict the perceived experience measures using both personality traits and nonverbal cues. The motivation for our study comes from several facts. As explained beforehand, personality traits shape perception and behaviors of humans in human-human and human-agent interaction. Nonverbal cues have been also shown to characterize several social constructs [13], and to be significant in predicting some of the Big 5 traits in social computing (e.g. in social media [3], and in face-to-face meetings [1]). Moreover, recent advances in social computing have shown how fusion of audio-visual data is significant for prediction of various behavioral patterns and phenomena in social dialogue, such as dominance [25] or aggression [14]. Thus, we believe that fusion of both visual and acoustic cues could be significant for predicting perceived measures of HAI. Our study is similar to the study with the Rapport agent [28], but with one major difference: rather than only observing the influence of personality traits on HAI experience we focus on the multi-modal analysis of perceived experience using both visual and vocal nonverbal behavior cues as well as the personality traits.

Specifically, in this paper we investigate the nonverbal cues and self-reported Big five traits as descriptors of an interaction of a person with two different virtual agents. We design a study in which we collect audio-visual data of humans talking with agents, along with their Big 5 traits and perceived experience measures. We describe interaction experience through three measures (quality, rapport and likeness) [7]. The virtual agents we use in our study are Sensitive Artificial Listeners (SALs)[17], which are designed with the purpose of inducing specific emotional conversation. There are in total four different agents in the SAL system: happy, angry, sad and neutral character. Studies suggest that the perceived personality of a social artifact has a significant effect on usability and acceptance [27], so we find these agents relevant to explore the interaction experience. Though SALs' understanding capabilities are limited to emotional processing, their personality has been successfully recognized in a recent evaluation study [17].

Our study has three contributions. First, we examine the relation between the self-reported Big 5 traits and perceived experience in human-agent interaction, with comparison to existing work in social psychology and human-agent interaction. Second, we investigate links between nonverbal cues and perceived experience, with an aim to find which nonverbal patterns are significant descriptors of experience aspects: quality of interaction, rapport and likeness of the agent. Finally, we build a method to predict HAI experience outcome based on automatically extracted nonverbal cues displayed during the interaction and self-reported Big 5 traits. Given the fact that we record our subjects with a consumer depth camera, we also investigate and discuss potentials of using cheap markerless tracking system for analyzing nonverbal behaviors.

2   Data Collection

Our data collection contains recordings of 33 subjects, out of which are 14 females and 19 males. 26 are graduate students and researchers in computer science, and

Fig. 1. Recording environment with a participant

7 are students of management. Most of them have different cultural background; however 85% subjects are Caucasians. Subjects were recruited using two mailing lists and they were compensated with 10 CHF for participation.

Before the recording session, each subject had to sign the consent form, and fill out demographic information and NEO FFI Big 5 personality questionnaire [16]. The recording session contains three recordings of the subject, where the data has been captured with a Kinect RGB-D camera (see Figure 1). First, the subject was asked to give a 1-minute self-presentation via video call. Then, he/she had two 4-minute interactions with two agents: first interaction was with sad Obadiah, and second with cheerful Poppy. These characters are selected because evaluation study on SALs [17] has shown how Poppy is the most consistent and familiar and Obadiah is the most believable character. Before the interaction, subjects were given an explanation what SALs are and what they can expect from interaction. To encourage the interaction, a list of potential conversation topics was placed in the view-field of a subject. Topics were: plans for the weekend, vacation plans, things that a subject did yesterday/last weekend, country where a subject was born, last book which a subject read. After each human-agent interaction, the subjects filled out a questionnaire, reporting their perceived interaction experience and mood. Due to the relatively small number of recruited subjects, we assigned all subjects to same experimental conditions, meaning that they first interacted with sad Obadiah, then to cheerful Poppy.

Interaction experience measures have been inspired from the study [7] in which authors investigate how Big 5 traits are manifested in mixed-sex dyadic interactions of strangers. To measure perceived interaction, they construct a "Perception of Interaction" questionnaire with items which rate various aspects of participants' interaction experience. We target the same aspects in human-agent interaction: Quality of Interaction (QoI), Degree of Rapport (DoR) and Degree of Likeness of the agent (DoL). Each interaction aspect in our questionnaire was targeted by a group of statements with a five-point Likert scale ((1) - Disagree strongly to (5) - Agree strongly).

Some of the items used by [7] were excluded, such as "I believe that partner wants to interact more in the future", given the constrained social and perception abilities of SALs. In total, our interaction questionnaire has 15 items which report QoI (7), DoR (5) and DoL (3). The questions that we used in the questionnaire and the target aspect of each question is shown in Table 1. The values of these measures are normalized to the range in $[0, 1]$. Additionally, our questionnaire also measures subject's mood (same questionnaire as used in [4]), which is at the moment excluded from our experiments.

Table 1. The questions and targeted aspects in the interaction questionnaire

Question	Target Aspect
The interaction with the character was smooth, natural, and relaxed.	QoI
I felt accepted and respected by the character.	DoR
I think the character is likable.	DoL
I enjoyed the interaction	QoI.
I got along with the character pretty good.	DoR
The interaction with the character was forced, awkward, and strained.	QoI
I did not want to get along with the character.	DoL
I was paying attention to way that character responds to me and I was adapting my own behaviour to it.	DoR
I felt uncomfortable during the interaction.	QoI
The character often said things completely out of place.	QoI
I think that the character finds me likable.	DoR
The interaction with the character was pleasant and interesting.	QoI
I would like to interact more with the character in the future.	DoL
I felt that character was paying attention to my mood.	DoR
I felt self-conscious during the conversation.	QoI

At the end of each recording session, several streams were obtained: RGB-D data and audio data from Kinect, and screen captures and log files with description of agent's behaviour.

3   Cue Extraction

We extracted nonverbal cues from both visual and auditory channel. The selection of features was based on previous studies on human-human interaction and conversational displays in psychology. For visual nonverbal displays we studied the literature on displays of attitude in initial human-human interactions (interactions where the interaction partners meet for the first time). Then, given the fact that previous research has shown how personality traits of extraversion and agreeableness are important predictors of HAI [28], we also take into account findings on nonverbal cues which are important for predicting personality traits.

Related to attitude in initial human-human interaction, a number of works observe how postural congruence and mimicry are positively related to liking and rapport ([15,31], or more recently [29]). Mimicry has also been investigated in human-agent community, with attempts to build automatic models to predict mimicry [26]. Our interaction scenario can only observe facial mimicry, because SAL agents have only their face visible and they do not make any body leans. Among other nonverbal cues, psychological literature agrees how frequent eye contact, relaxation, leaning and orienting towards, less fiddling, moving closer, touching, more open arm and leg positions, smiling and more expressive face and voice are signs of liking from observer's (or coder's) point of view [2,13]. Yet, when it comes to displays of liking associated with self-reported measures, findings are not that evident. In an extensive review of literature dealing with the posture cue, Mehrabian shows how displays of liking vary from gender and status [18]. He also shows how larger reclining angle of sideways leaning communicates a more negative attitude, and smaller reclining angle of a communicator while seated, and therefore a smaller degree of trunk relaxation, communicates a more positive attitude. Investigation of non-verbal behavior cues and liking conducted on initial same-sex dyad interactions [15] shows how the most significant variables in predicting subjects' liking is the actual amount of mutual gaze and the total percentage time looking. Other significant behaviors are: expressiveness of the face and the amount of activity in movement and gesture, synchrony of movement and speech, and expressiveness of the face and gesturing. Another cross-study [24] examined only kinesics and vocalic behaviors. Results show how increased pitch variety is associated with female actors, whereas interesting effect is noticed for loudness and length of talking, which decrease over interaction time. Though authors say how their research shows how this means disengagement in conversations, another work reports how this means greater attractiveness [21].

Psychologists have noted that, when observed alone, vocal and paralinguistic features have the highest correlation with person judgments of personality traits, at least in certain experimental conditions [8]. This has been confirmed in some studies in automatic recognition of personality traits which use nonverbal behavior as predictors. A study on the prediction of personality impressions analyses predictability of Big 5 personality trait impressions using audio-visual nonverbal cues extracted from the vlogs [3]. Nonverbal cues include speaking activity (speaking time, pauses, etc.), prosody (spectral entropy, pitch, etc.), motion (weigthed motion energy images, movements in front of camera), gaze behavior, vertical framing (position of the face), and distance to camera. Among the cues, speaking time and length, prosody, motion and looking time were most significant for inferring the perceived personality. Observer judgments of extraversion are positively correlated with high fluency, meaning greater length of the speech segments, and less number of speaking turns, and positively with loudness, looking time and motion. People who are observed as more agreeable speak with higher voice, and people who are observed as more extraverted have a higher vocal control. In another study on meeting videos [23], speech related measurements (e.g., speaking time, mean energy, pitch, etc.) and percent of looking time (e.g., amount of received and given gaze) were shown as significant predictors of personality traits.

Based on the overviewed literature we extract the following features from human-agent interaction sequences: speaking activity, prosody, body leans, head direction, visual activity, and hand activity. Every cue, except hand activity, is extracted automatically from whole conversational sequences. Whereas we acknowledge the importance of mimicry, in this experiment we only extract individual behaviors of humans without looking at agent's behavior.

3.1   Audio Cues

To extract nonverbal cues from speech, we first applied automatic speaker diarization on human-agent audio files using Idiap Speaker Diarization Toolkit [30]. We further used MIT Human Dynamics group toolkit ([22] to export voice quality measures.

Speaking Activity. Based on the diarization output, we extracted the speech segments of the subject and computed the following features for each human-agent sequence: total speaking length (TSL), total speaking turns (TST), filtered turns, and average turn duration (ATD).

Voice Quality Measures. The voice quality measures are extracted on the subject's speech, based on the diarization output. We extracted the statistics - mean and standard deviation - of following features: pitch (F0 (m), F0 (std)), pitch confidence (F0 conf (m), F0 conf (std)), spectral entropy (SE (m), SE (std)), delta energy (DE (m), DE (std)), location of autocorrelation peaks (Loc R0 (m), Loc R0 (std), number of autocorrelation peaks (# R0 (m), # R0 (std)), value of of autocorrelation peaks (Val R0 (m), Val R0 (std)). Furthermore, three other measures were exported: average length of speaking segment (ALSS), average length of voiced segment (ALVS), fraction of time speaking (FTS), voicing rate (VR), and fraction speaking over (FSO).

3.2   Visual Cues

One of the aspects we wanted to investigate in this study is the potential of using cheap markerless motion capture systems (MS Kinect SDK v1.8) for the purpose of automatic social behavior analysis. Using Kinect SDK upper body and face tracking information we created body lean and head direction classifier. Since the tracker produced significantly poor results for arm/hand joints, hand activity of the subject during the interaction was manually annotated.

Body Leans. In this paper we propose a module for automatic analysis of body leans from 3D upper body pose and depth image. We use a support vector machine (SVM) classifier, RBF kernel, trained with extended 3D upper body pose features. Extended 3D upper body pose is an extended version of features extracted from Kinect SDK upper body tracker; along with x-y position values of shoulders, neck and head, it also contains torso information and z-values of shoulders, neck and torso normalized with respect to the neutral body pose. Using our classifier, distribution of the following body leans is extracted: neutral, sideways left, sideways right (SR), forward and backward leans (BL). These categories are inspired from psychological work on posture behavior and displays of affect [18]. Along with those distributions we also compute frequency of shifting between those leans.

Head Direction. We use a simple method which outputs three head directions; screen, table, or other (HDO), and frequency of shifts (HDFS). The method is using 3D object approximation of screen and table and head information retrieved from Kinect face tracker. The method is tested on manually annotated ground truth data and is proven to produce satisfying results.

Visual Activity. The visual activity of the subject is extracted by using weighted motion energy images (wMEI), which is a binary image that describes the spatial motion distribution in the video sequence [3]. The features we extract are statistics of wMEI: entropy, mean and median value.

Hand Activity. To manually annotate hand activity we used the following classes: hidden hands, hand gestures (GES), gestures on table, hands on table, and self-touch (ST). The classes are proposed in a study on body expressions of participants of employment interviews [20].

4   Analysis and Results

In the first two parts of this section, we present the correlation analysis and links between the interaction experience and Big 5 traits and also the extracted nonverbal cues. We compare and discuss our results with previous works from psychology and human-agent interaction literature. We also present the results of our experiments for predicting interaction experience.

4.1   Personality and Interaction Experience

We find the individual correlations between Big 5 traits of the participants and individual measures of interaction experience to understand what traits may be useful to infer interaction with two virtual characters.

Table 2 shows the significant correlations. Extraversion has the highest correlations with both agents; it is then followed by neuroticism and agreeableness. With regard to extraversion, we found that extraverted subjects reported good QoI and high DoR to both of agents. Extraverted people also reported high DoL for Obadiah, whereas for Poppy we found no significant evidence. In a study on human-human interaction which inspired our work ([7]) the extraverted people were more likely to report that they did not feel self-conscious, they perceived their interaction to be smooth, natural, and relaxed, and they felt comfortable around their interaction partner. The similar study on Big Five manifestation in initial dyadic interactions[9] has also shown how extraverted people tend to rate interaction natural and relaxed. This is a direct reference to Carl Jungs view

Table 2. Significant Pearson correlation effects between Big Five traits and interaction experience measures: QoI, DoR and DoL (p <0.05,*p <0.01)

	Obadiah	Poppy
Openness to Exp.	-	-
Conscientiousness	QoI (.41)	-
Extraversion	QoI (.44) DoR (.58)* DoL (.42)	QoI (.36) DoR (.44)
Agreeableness	DoR (.47)*	DoR (.46)*
Neuroticism	DoR (.40)	QoI (.37) DoR (.45)* DoL (.44)

that extraverts' attention is directed outward, away from themselves [11]. These results for extraversion show how social psychology research is translated to the context of human-agent interaction. With regard to agreeableness, we found that more agreeable subjects reported higher DoR to both agents, which is also supported by [7], and to existing work in human-agent interaction and perception of rapport [12], which is not surprising, since agreeableness is associated with friendliness, warmth, and sociability. People with higher degree of neuroticism reported higher DoR, QoI and DoL only to agent Poppy. People high in conscientiousness reported higher QoI only for sad Obadiah. With regard to openness to experience, no significant results can be reported.

We would also like to drive comparison of our results to existing work on the influence of extraversion trait on the perception of virtual characters with respect to similarity rule, and opposite, complementary rule introduced in Section 1. Our results show two correlation effects of DoL and Big 5 traits for both agents: Obadiah, who is shown to have high neuroticism, and Poppy, who is shown to have high extraversion [17]. Extraverted people in our study show tendency to like Obadiah (for Poppy no relation is found), whereas more people with high neuroticism show tendency to like Poppy (for Obadiah no relation is found). These results show support for the complementary likeness rule.

4.2   Nonverbal Cues and Interaction Experience

We study the individual association between nonverbal features and measures of interaction experience, which are shown in Table 3. As a first result we found that interactions with agent Poppy results in higher cue utilization (18) than with agent Obadiah (10). One possible, albeit speculative, explanation for this could be that subjects freely expressed themselves in second interaction (with Poppy) because they knew what is expected from them. This has been confirmed for assessment of personality meaning that 'when strangers get to know each other, information contained early in the interaction may be less useful for making accurate personality assessments' (see [17], p. 315. for discussion).

Table 3. Significant Pearson correlation effects between interaction experience measures and nonverbal cues (p <0.05, *p <0.01), see cue acronyms in Section 3.2

	Obadiah	Poppy
QoI	ATD (-.35), ALSS (-.35)	TSL (.41), TST (.48)*
	GES (-.36)	F0 (m) (-.40), Val R0 (m) (.37),
		Loc R0 (m) (-.35), ALVS (-.36)
		HDO (-.35), BL (-.49)*
	# Cues: 3	# Cues: 8
DoR	ATD (-.36)	TST (.36), Val R0 (m) (.37),
	ALSS (-.49)*	BL (-.47)*, SR (-.35), ST (-.46)*
	BL (-.42)	HDO (-.49)*, HDS (.38)
	# Cues: 3	# Cues: 7
DoL	ATD (-.35)	Loc R0 (std) (-.35)
	ALSS (-.51)*, FTS (-.41)	ALVS (-.36)
	FSO (-.41)	HDO (-.38)
	# Cues: 4	# Cues: 3

Another possible explanation of this phenomena could lie in design of our study: self-reported interaction measures in second interaction (with Poppy) could be affected by subject's experience and measures reported after interaction with Obadiah. The issues and proposed solutions are discussed in Conclusions section.

With regards to QoI, we expected that audio cues will be more significant than visual cues we extracted, as we do not take into account any facial expressions (e.g. confuse or surprise). This was the case, more significant for agent Poppy, with results showing that longer speaking time and more turns mean higher QoI, which is not surprising, taking into account that SALs are designed to induce interaction. Besides, lower pitch, higher value of autocorrelation peaks (louder speech), lower location of autocorrelation peaks, and lower average length of voiced segment also show higher QoI for Poppy. Among visual cues, back leans and head oriented away were found to be significant. Results show how people who lean back more and 'look away from screen' more are not having high QoI with Poppy. Back leans in this case may indicate boredom or lack of interest, whereas gaze in psychological literature serves both as regulator of conversation flow and indicator of attitude. Several studies have confirmed how frequent amount and length of gazing communicates positive attitude towards conversational partner (see [15] for an overview), so in our case, more frequent head directed outwards may also indicate lack of interest. Although in our case only head direction is computed, our results show that it is an acceptable approximation to eye contact in this scenario. For Obadiah QoI, we also got three significant results, showing that people who make less gestures and whose speech segments and turns last shorter are reporting higher QoI. Shorter speech segments and average turn duration, which are also reported for higher DoL and DoR for Obadiah, indicate that the interaction is indeed two ways, the agent responses to the subject, which could explain the high QoI. After the experiment, some subjects reported how 'they wanted to cheer up Obadiah', so these features could also indicate how subjects who reported higher QoI, DoR and DoL felt an empathy with sad Obadiah. To support this theory, linguistic content of the speech could be analyzed.

For Obadiah, people who also lean back a lot show lower DoR. In case of Poppy, people who take more turns, lean back less, lean sideways right less, speak louder, touch themselves less, look away from screen less show higher DoR. These can all be identified as signals of interest. These features are also found to be significant in human-human interaction ([7,15,18]). Though, in case of sideways leans Mehrabian argues how reclining angle is important to differentiate positive and negative attitude.

With regards to DoL, in the case of Obadiah, only vocal features of the subjects were found to be significant. Average turn duration, average length of speaking segments, lower fraction of speaking time and fraction speaking over are related to higher DoL, which means people who speak less tend to like Obadiah more. With regards to visual nonverbal cues and DoL, we found only one significant result only for Poppy. People who like Poppy more, do not move their head away from screen a lot. This result is also related to findings on likeness in human-human interaction, showing how people show more direct eye contact to liked partner [24].

4.3   Regression Analysis

The task of predicting the interaction experience is addressed by building computational models for predicting the score of individual measures of perceived experience: QoI, DoR and DoL. For prediction task we used three different regression models: support vector regression (SVR), neural networks (NN) and kernel ridge regression (KRR). Each model is trained using double cross-validation (CV) approach in which for outer fold we used leave-one-out CV, and for inner fold we used 5-fold CV approach. The inner fold is used for parameter optimization. SVR and KRR models use RBF kernel. The models are trained with different feature sets: we experimented with (1) all extracted nonverbal behavior (NVB) cues, (2) all NVB cues and all personality traits (PT), (3) all PT, (4) significant NVB cues, (5) significant PT, and (6) significant NVB and PT (significant NVB cues and PT are shown in tables 2 and 3). Additionally, for all feature sets we also applied Principal Component Analysis (PCA), in order to reduce dimensionality of data.

Table 4 shows the results of our experiments, where we report the R^2 and Root Mean Square Error (RMSE). Among different feature sets and regression models that we have experimented with, we report the best results for each experience aspect. To stress the difference between experimented feature sets, we only show the results of the best regression model for a specific feature set.

One can first notice how for the best results are obtained when personality traits and nonverbal cues are combined, which boost the performance of each individual input source (PT and NVB used alone). QoI and DoR for both agents are predicted with R^2 of 0.3. Although the R^2 values found for QoI and DoR are on the low side, they are comparable to the results found in other studies

Table 4. Prediction results for Obadiah and Poppy with different feature sets (Personality traits (PT), nonverbal behavior (NVB), all vs. significant cues. For each feature set we only show results of the best regression model.

		Feature Set	Meth.	R2	RMSE
Obadiah	QoI	NVB+PT (sig.)	SVR	0.292	0.144
		PT (sig.)	SVR	0.158	0.157
		NVB+PT (all, PCA)	SVR	0.034	0.168
	DoR	NVB+PT (sig.)	SVR	0.34	0.137
		PT (sig.)	KRR	0.134	0.156
		NVB (sig.)	KRR	0.106	0.159
	DoL	NVB+PT (sig)	KRR	0.174	0.197
		NVB (sig.)	KRR	0.066	0.209
		PT (sig.)	SVR	0.016	0.215
Poppy	QoI	NVB+PT (sig.)	KRR	0.523	0.129
		NVB (sig.)	KRR	0.158	0.172
		PT (sig.)	SVR	0.015	0.186
	DoR	NVB+PT (sig.)	KRR	0.406	0.162
		NVB (sig)	KRR	0.158	0.192
		NVB+PT (all, PCA)	KRR	0.114	0.199
	DoL	NVB+PT (sig.)	SVR	0.322	0.200
		NVB+PT (all, PCA)	KRR	0.097	0.230

in social computing literature for predicting several other social aspects such as personality [1,3]. DoL is the weakest aspect of our prediction models: The highest R^2 for Obadiah is 0.174 and Poppy 0.322. With regards to the regression method, SVR and KRR have shown to produce similar results and they outperformed NN.

5 Conclusions

Our paper presented a study in which we attempt to analyze and predict the experience of interaction (or perceived interaction) with virtual characters. A novelty of our work is that we use a combination of nonverbal cues and personality traits to predict the experience. Best prediction results for all experience measures were obtained when nonverbal cues and personality traits are used together as features. The degree of rapport for agent Obadiah and quality of interaction for agent Poppy are the most predictable measures.

We examined self-reported personality traits and extracted nonverbal cues as descriptors of experience and found that personality traits are very significant features, as also reported in [28]. This is another confirmation how humans' personality shapes the experience of human-agent interaction, and how it should be assessed in virtual agents evaluation studies. Another finding related to our work shows how people with high agreeableness perceive strong rapport with an agent designed to build rapport [12]. Our results however suggest that characterization of an agent might not play a role in perceiving the rapport during interaction.

People who score high in agreeableness in our study reported higher rapport with both sad Obadiah and cheerful Poppy. This also points to prior findings on human-human interaction on how the presence of at least one agreeable member in the dyad results with higher rapport perceived with conversational partner [7]. We have also found that some of the extracted nonverbal features significant for describing experience are related to socio-psychological findings on affect and liking, such as body leaning and head orientation. Acoustic and paraliguistic features were shown as more meaningful descriptors than visual features, which is also phenomena observed for judgments of personality traits [8]. All nonverbal features, except hand activities are automatically exported. Cheap markerless motion capture system (MS Kinect v1.8) was found to be partially useful for the purpose of automatic social behavior analysis. Experiments with head information from the face tracking system were successful and we build head direction classifier. However, in subjective evaluation upper body tracking failed to produce reliable results for hand joints so hand activity was manually annotated. Moreover, additional information was required to build body-lean classifier from body tracking system.

A limitation of our study is experimental design. Limited by resources, we assigned our subjects to the same experimental conditions, in which they first completed the interaction with Obadiah, and then for Poppy. The questionnaire was applied after each interaction. One could expect that experience of the second interaction is affected by the first interaction. The same fact is the reason why we can not strongly support complementary likeness rule in HAI, which is suggested by our results. Besides, it has been observed how more significant nonverbal features, or higher cue utilization for interaction scores, were found in second interaction. As explained beforehand, subjects might have freely expressed themselves because they got accustomed to the SAL system.

To overcome somewhat arguable interaction scores we plan to crowdsource the annotation of observed experience from collected audio-visual data. Then, we will perform a study on comparison of self-reported and observed measures. Moreover, to improve prediction of experience additional nonverbal features are considered to be exported: to improve prediction of likeness e.g. eye shifts and eye contact could be useful [24], and to improve quality of interaction overlapped speech segments could be significant. Instead of using self-reported personality scores as inputs of our regression models, we plan to build computational models which predict personality from audio-visual data. For this task, a thorough study on prediction of personality from nonverbal cues from both human-agent interaction and self-presentation sequences will be done.

Acknowledgments. This work was partly funded by the Swiss National Science Foundation (SNSF) Ambizione project "Multimodal Computational Modeling of Nonverbal Social Behavior in Face to Face Interaction" (PZ00P2-136811) and by grants from the Croatian Science Foundation (CSF), and Pascal 2 Network of Excellence.

References

1. Aran, O., Gatica-Perez, D.: One of a Kind: Inferring Personality Impressions in Meetings. In: International Conference on Multimodal Interaction (ICMI), Sydney, pp. 11–18 (2013)
2. Argyle, M.: Bodily communication. Methuen (1988)
3. Biel, J.-I., Gatica-Perez, D.: The Youtube lens: Crowdsourced personality impression and audiovisual of vlogs. IEEE Transactions on Multimedia 15(1), 41–55 (2012)
4. Biel, J.-I., Aran, O., Gatica-Perez, D.: The Good, the Bad, and the Angry: Analyzing Crowdsourced Impressions of Vloggers. In: International Conference on Weblogs and Social Media, ICWSM (2012)
5. Buisine, S., Martin, J.C.: The influence of user's personality and gender on the processing of virtual agents multimodal behavior. Advances in Psychology Research, 1–14 (2010)
6. Cafaro, A., Vilhjálmsson, H.H., Bickmore, T., Heylen, D., Jóhannsdóttir, K.R., Valgardhsson, G.S.: First impressions: Users' judgments of virtual agents' personality and interpersonal attitude in first encounters. In: Nakano, Y., Neff, M., Paiva, A., Walker, M. (eds.) IVA 2012. LNCS, vol. 7502, pp. 67–80. Springer, Heidelberg (2012)
7. Cuperman, R., Ickes, W.: Big five predictors of behavior and perceptions in initial dyadic interactions: personality similarity helps extraverts and introverts, but hurts disagreeables. Journal of Personality and Social Psychology 97(4), 667–684 (2009)
8. Ekman, P., Friesen, W., O'Sullivan, M., Cherer, K.: Relative importance of face, body, and speech in judgments of personality and affect. Journal of Personality and Social Psychology 38(2), 270–277 (1980)
9. Funder, D.C., Sneed, C.D.: Behavioral manifestations of personality: An ecological approach to judgmental accuracy. Journal of Personality and Social Psychology 64, 479–490 (1993)
10. Isbister, K., Nass, C.: Consistency of personality in interactive characters: verbal cues, non-verbal cues, and user characteristics. International Journal of Human-Computer Studies 53(2), 251–267 (2000)
11. Jung, C.: Psychological types. Harcourt, Brace, New York (1921)
12. Kang, S.-H., Gratch, J., Wang, N., Watt, J.H.: Agreeable people like agreeable virtual humans. In: Prendinger, H., Lester, J.C., Ishizuka, M. (eds.) IVA 2008. LNCS (LNAI), vol. 5208, pp. 253–261. Springer, Heidelberg (2008)
13. Knapp, M.L., Hall, J.A., Horgan, T.G.: Nonverbal Communication in Human Interaction, 8th edn. Cengage Learning (January 2013)
14. Lefter, I., Burghouts, G.J., Rothkrantz, L.J.M.: Automatic Audio-Visual Fusion for Aggression Detection Using Meta-information avss. In: 2012 IEEE Ninth International Conference on Advanced Video and Signal-Based Surveillance, pp. 19–24 (2012)
15. Maxwell, G.M., Cook, M.W.: Postural congruence and judgements of liking and perceived similarity. New Zealand Journal of Psychology 15(1), 20–26 (1985)
16. McCrae, R.R., Costa, P.T.: A contemplated revision of the NEO Five-Factor Inventory. Personality and Individual Differences 36(3), 587–596 (2004)
17. McRorie, M., Sneddon, I., McKeown, G., Bevacqua, E., Sevin, E., Pelachaud, C.: Evaluation of four designed virtual agent personalities. Transactions on Affective Computing 3(3), 311–322 (2012)

18. Mehrabian, A.: Significance of posture and position in the communication of attitude and status relationships. Psychological Bulletin 71(5), 359–372 (1969)
19. Nass, C., Lee, K.M.: Does computer-generated speech manifest personality? an experimental test of similarity-attraction. In: CHI 2000: Proceedings of the SIGCHI Conference on Human Factors in Computing Systems, New York, NY, USA, pp. 329–336 (2000)
20. Nguyen, L., Marcos-Ramiro, A., Marron-Romera, M., Gatica-Perez, D.: Multimodal Analysis of Body Communication Cues in Employment Interviews. In: Proc. ACM Int. Conf. on Multimodal Interaction (ICMI), Sydney (December 2013)
21. Palmer, M.T., Simmons, K.B.: Communicating intentions through nonverbal behaviors conscious and nonconscious encoding of liking. Human Communication Research 22(1), 128–160 (1995)
22. Pentland, A.S.: Honest Signals: How They Shape Our World. The MIT Press (2008)
23. Pianesi, F., Zancanaro, M., Lepri, B., Cappelletti, A.: A multimodal annotated corpus of consensus decision making meetings. Language Resources and Evaluation 41(3), 409–429 (2007)
24. Ray, G.B., Floyd, K.: Nonverbal expressions of liking and disliking in initial interaction: Encoding and decoding perspectives. Southern Communication Journal 71(1), 45–65 (2006)
25. Sanchez-Cortes, D., Aran, O., Jayagopi, D., Schmid Mast, M., Gatica-Perez, D.: Emergent Leaders through Looking and Speaking: From Audio-Visual Data to Multimodal Recognition. Journal on Multimodal User Interfaces Special Issue on Multimodal Corpora 7(1-2), 39–53 (2013) (published online August 2012)
26. Sun, X., Nijholt, A., Truong, K.P., Pantic, M.: Automatic understanding of affective and social signals by multimodal mimicry recognition. In: D'Mello, S., Graesser, A., Schuller, B., Martin, J.-C. (eds.) ACII 2011, Part II. LNCS, vol. 6975, pp. 289–296. Springer, Heidelberg (2011)
27. Tapus, A., Mataric, M.J.: Socially assistive robots: The link between personality, empathy, physiological signals, and task performance. In: Emotion, Personality, and Social Behavior, pp. 133–140. AAAI (2008)
28. von der Pütten, A.M., Krämer, N.C., Gratch, J.: How our personality shapes our interactions with virtual characters - implications for research and development. In: Safonova, A. (ed.) IVA 2010. LNCS, vol. 6356, pp. 208–221. Springer, Heidelberg (2010)
29. Vacharkulksemsuk, T.B., Fredrickson, L.: Strangers in sync: Achieving embodied rapport through shared movements. Journal of Experimental Social Psychology 48(1), 399–402 (2012)
30. Vijayasenan, D., Valente, F., Bourlard, H.: An Information Theoretic Combination of MFCC and TDOA Features for Speaker Diarization. IEEE Transactions on Audio Speech and Language Processing 19(2) (2011)
31. Waldron, J.: Judgement of like-dislike from facial expression and body posture. Perceptual and Motor Skills 41(3), 799–804 (1975)

Human Involvement in E-Coaching:
Effects on Effectiveness, Perceived Influence and Trust

Bart A. Kamphorst[1], Michel C.A. Klein[2], and Arlette van Wissen[2],[*]

[1] Utrecht University, Dept. of Philosophy and Religious Studies
Janskerkhof 13A, 3512 BL Utrecht
b.a.kamphorst@uu.nl
[2] VU University Amsterdam, Dept. of Computer Science
De Boelelaan 1085, 1081 HV Amsterdam, The Netherlands
{michel.klein,a.van.wissen}@vu.nl

Abstract. Coaching practices are rapidly changing due to advances in pervasive computing: behavior of coachees can unobtrusively be monitored in real time, and coaching can be remote or even fully automated. Fully autonomous e-coaching systems hold promise for improving people's self-management, but also raise questions about the importance of human involvement in the e-coaching process. This paper describes an empirical 'Wizard of Oz' study in which coachees (N=82) were coached to take the stairs by either another person (N=20) or the e-coaching system eMate. Crucially, some coachees were made to believe that they would receive one type of coaching (human or computerized), while in reality they received the other. Results show that the coaching was equally effective in all groups, but that people who believed to be coached by a human judged the coaching to be more influential. No difference was found between groups in how trustworthy coachees found their coaches.

1 Introduction

Many people struggle to change and improve their behavior. As behavior is influenced by habits, biases, and unconscious responses, people can often benefit from *coaching*. Advances in pervasive technologies are causing coaching practices to change. The emergence of 'smart environments' and mobile platforms is enabling the development of ambient, autonomous "e-coaching" systems, which, due to their characteristics of being mobile, adaptive and context-aware, show increasing promise for supporting people in their everyday life.

Autonomous e-coaching systems (hereinafter, e-coaching systems) are a class of decision support systems designed to assist people with self-improvement in a variety of areas [28]. In the foreseeable future, e-coaching systems are likely to increase in prevalence, due to low costs and a level of anonymity that many people favor (see [7]). However, this development is not without concerns (for discussion, see [1] and [10]). Because coach-coachee relationships are of crucial importance for effective coaching [9], it may be questioned whether e-coaching systems could really fulfill a full-fledged

---

[*] All authors contributed equally to this work.

H.S. Park et al. (Eds.): HBU 2014, LNCS 8749, pp. 16–29, 2014.

coaching role, or whether they would miss 'that particular human quality' that makes for good coaching relationships. This, then, raises the question: What influence does human involvement in e-coaching actually have?

This paper describes an empirical 'Wizard of Oz' study on computer-mediated coaching that evaluates the effect of the coaching system eMate [12] on human behavior. This experiment, which involves a deception about the type of coaching that participants received, tests whether people have different coaching experiences when being coached by a computer rather than by a human being. The details of the experimental design are described in Section 4. The application domain is healthy lifestyle improvement by stimulating people to take the stairs more often. This domain was chosen because it has a clean outcome measure (the number of stairs taken, where stairs are defined as all the steps between two floors) and because the choice between stairs and elevator is one that people often face in their daily lives.

This work focuses on three outcome measures: the effectiveness of the coaching, the perceived influence of the coaching (as judged by coachees), and the trust that coachees developed in their coaches. With regard to these measures we formulated three hypotheses. First, the belief that coachees have about the identity of their coach (human or computer) will have no effect on effectiveness. That is, coaching by eMate and coaching by a human will lead to an equal degree of behavior change. Second, the belief that coachees have about the identity of their coach (human or computer) will have no effect on how influential coachees consider the intervention. And third, the belief that coachees have about the identity of their coach (human or computer) will have no effect on trust. The motivations for these hypotheses are discussed in Section 2.

Results show that all groups improved in comparable measure (although there was no significant improvement for the entire sample of coachees), which confirms hypothesis 1. This indicates that e-coaching can be employed without the (transparent) involvement of a human coach. Interestingly, contrary to hypothesis 2, coachees did judge the intervention to be more influential if they believed to be coached by a human being. With regard to trust however, no differences were found between groups, confirming hypothesis 3.

2   Related Work

The largest body of work on how people perceive computers comes from Nass (e.g., [21], [8], [17]). His work on the "media equation" provides evidence that people treat computers as social actors, no other than they would treat other human beings. Reeves and Nass found that people unconsciously and automatically apply social rules when they interact with computers and other media [21]. This has been shown to hold for instance with regard to human factors such as flattery [8] and politeness [17]. Work by Van Wissen, Van Diggelen, and Dignum corroborates these findings in showing that people exhibit similar levels of reciprocity towards humans and computer agents [27]. Additionally, in an experiment on team formation in dynamic environments with uncertainty, people have been shown to be as loyal to agent-led teams as to human-led teams [26]. It was also shown that people prefer to create teams with others with whom they have had positive interactions (humans and agents alike), rather than those who offer them large rewards. Work by Bickmore and Picard further demonstrates that factors such as trust play an important role when designing for long-term interaction — which is particularly relevant for personal coaching — and that increased trust leads to a greater desire to continue the interactions [3]. With regard to trust, it was found that people generally trust computers in a way that is similar to the way they trust humans [14, 19].

These findings together suggest that people's interactions with computer coaches will be similar to the interactions they have with human coaches. Other work, however, suggests some nuances to this claim for specific domains. For example, Blount showed that in an ultimatum game people are more likely to accept lower offers from computers than from human proposers [4]. According to Van Dongen and Van Maanen, there is an asymmetry in how people attribute trust to themselves and to decision aids [25]. In addition, it has been shown that people do treat computers differently in team settings with regard to fairness considerations [26].

Although the mentioned literature shows some differences for several social factors between human-human interaction and human-computer interaction, the present work does not involve these particular factors (negotiation, fairness, and choosing teammates). Hypotheses 1 and 2 are therefore based on the findings that showed similar social relations between humans and computers and between humans and humans. Furthermore, the computer system in the current experiment is not a mere decision aid (giving advice based on probabilities, algorithms and calculations), but relies on persuasive strategies and repeated interaction to support behavior change. Hypothesis 3 therefore assumes that the social role of the e-coaching system will trigger similar trust responses in interactions with eMate to interactions with a human being.

3   eMate

The eMate system is an intelligent coaching system that uses both mobile phone applications and a website to interact with the user [13]. The system performs the following tasks: (1) it determines the *stage of change* of a user, (2) it *monitors* the behavior of the user to determine the level of goal adherence, (3) it *reasons* about the changes required for improvement, (4) it tries to *change the user's perception* of specific aspects of behavior change, and (5) it *updates* its beliefs about the user. The monitoring is performed using a web-based system, a smartphone app (for presenting messages (see Fig. 1a) and asking questions (Fig. 1b)) and an optional electronic pillbox (not used in the present study).

The *stage of change* is a phase in the characterization of a behavior change process according to the Transtheoretical Model [18]. This model assumes that behavior change passes through five stages: *precontemplation, contemplation, preparation, action,* and *maintenance.* The content of eMate's interventions depends on the stage in which eMate determines that a person is.

At the core of eMate is the Computerized Behavior Intervention (COMBI) model [13], which integrates different theories of behavior change into a formal representation of a causal model. The eMate system uses the COMBI model to reason about underlying causes for non-adherence. It will determine what is preventing a user from moving

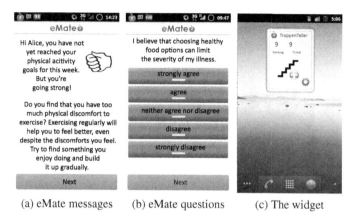

(a) eMate messages   (b) eMate questions   (c) The widget

Fig. 1. The eMate app and StairsCounter widget

to the next stage of change by investigating whether the constructs that influence the consecutive stage (i.e., the factors that are directly associated with this stage) are a *bottleneck*. In order to keep the information about the COMBI constructs up to date, eMate sends the user questions via the eMate app. The answers are used to update the values of the constructs. The intervention then targets the bottlenecks as determined by the reasoning process. That is, users will receive motivational and informative messages related to these constructs. This is done on a weekly basis.

Messages consist of three parts: a summary of the user's behavior based on the results of the monitoring, a motivational message targeting the bottleneck, and a concluding remark (comparable to the message format in [23]). Users thus get an update about the relation between their goals and their actual behavior, in addition to personalized persuasive messages.

An Android widget was developed for this study (shown in Fig. 1c), and the eMate website (see Fig. 2) and messages were tailored to the domain of taking the stairs in consultation with a communication expert who has experience with promoting stairs use. For more details on the COMBI model and the implementation of eMate, see [13].

4   Methods

Participants. The coachees (N=82, 41 female) were students of the VU University Amsterdam, aged between 15 and 30 (avg: 21 years). Upon agreeing to participate they were randomly assigned to a condition. The criterion for participation as a coachee was having a smartphone running Android (version 2.3.3+). The 'coaches' (N=20, 11 female) were recruited at Utrecht University and were between 19 and 34 years old (avg: 29 years). They had zero to some previous experience with coaching (65% and 35%, respectively). Note that the individuals who fulfilled this coaching role were not professional coaches. This lack of expertise was desirable, as they were assisted in their coaching role (as will be explained in Section 4), and we did not want to introduce a bias based on expertise. To appreciate this point, it is important to keep in mind that the

Fig. 2. The eMate website showing a picture of a building with an equivalent number of stairs as the participant has taken (here: the Rocky Steps)

aim of the study was to investigate whether the (mere) belief about human involvement alone makes a difference to the coaching. Both coaches and coachees were rewarded €10 for their efforts at the end of the study.

Design. The experiment used a 'Wizard of Oz' design: coachees received coaching from either eMate or a human coach, but in some conditions the coachees were deceived about the identity of their coach. In the experiment, all coachees received messages through the same Android app. To successfully keep up the deception, these messages were signed either with 'your eMate coach' or with a human name.[1]

There were four conditions in total, which are depicted in Fig. 3. The conditions are characterized by the *backend* that provides the coaching messages (either a human coach or the eMate system) and the *belief* dat participants have about the identity of their coach (human or computer). For instance, in condition 3, coachees were coached by eMate but made to believe they were being coached by a human coach. In addition to the four conditions, Fig. 3 shows four other (partly overlapping) groups. Group 5 consists of everyone who believed that their coach was human, and group 6 consists of everyone who believed that their coach was eMate. Groups 7 and 8 are grouped by the actual coaching backend (human or eMate).

The setup included a website (which provided coaches with a web form for writing messages and coachees with information about their stair climbing efforts), an Android widget for counting stairs (coachees only), an Android app for receiving questions and messages (coachees only), the eMate coaching engine, a database backend, and an email script for notifying coaches about their coaching tasks. An overview of the infrastructure can be found in Fig. 4.

Coachee Intake Survey.[2] The intake survey covered demographics; stages of change with respect to taking the stairs; knowledge, attitudes and habits of stairs use; and

---

[1] To prevent the introduction of a gender-related dimension into the experiment, names were chosen that could be both for a male or female coach (e.g., Robin, or Kris).

[2] All used surveys (in Dutch) can be found at http://bit.ly/stairs_surveys.

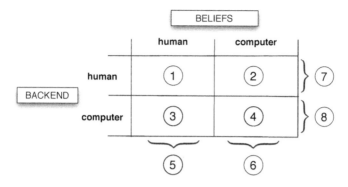

Fig. 3. Overview of the experimental conditions

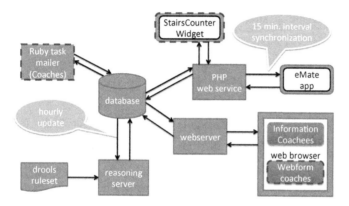

Fig. 4. Experimental infrastructure - image adapted from Klein et al. (2013), additions with dashed lines

enabling and disabling factors for taking the stairs. To determine the stage of change, questions were asked using a yes-no format in an algorithm adapted from [20], which is considered the most reliable and valid way to determine stage of change in the exercise domain. The questions were modified to focus on taking the stairs rather than on general exercise behavior. To establish the values for the determinants of the COMBI model, several validated questionnaires were used. An overview can be found in Table 1. For those determinants not in Table 1, either no validated questionnaire was available, or it was judged too lengthly (and therefore costly). Instead, questions for the remaining determinants were mostly taken from the original COMBI intake survey [13].

Coachee Evaluation Survey. At the end of the experiment, after four weeks of monitoring stairs use, the coachees were admitted an evaluation survey. The evaluation

Table 1. Used validated surveys to determine COMBI determinants

COMBI determinant	Survey	Source
skills	Utrecht Proactive Coping Competence List (short) (UPCC)	[5]
self-efficacy	Self-Efficacy Scale	[2]
mood	Subjective Exercise Experiences Scale (SEES)	[16]
coping	Coping Inventory for Stressful Situation (CISS-21)	[6]
motivation	Exercise Self-Regulation Questionnaire (SRQ-E)	[22]

survey addressed again the stage of change and the COMBI determinants. Some questions were added that addressed the deception component of the experiment, which is discussed in the results section. Also, some additional surveys were incorporated with the purpose of gaining insights into matters of user experience. The most important one for this paper is the measure of human-computer trust (HCT; [15]). This measure is specifically designed for intelligent systems that aid decision making and consists of five subscales: reliability, attachment, understandability, technical competence and faith.

Coach Surveys. Coaches were admitted short intake and evaluation surveys. The main objective of these surveys was to obtain knowledge of the coach's (i) demographics, (ii) previous coaching experience, and (iii) coaching style.

Procedure for Coaches. It was explained to coaches that for four weeks, they would coach other people by writing short, motivational messages in an online form. This form would guide the coaches in making suitable messages, by providing a relevant piece of information about taking the stairs (e.g., "Taking the stairs activates about 200 muscles"). The coaches were asked to use this information to compose their messages in their own words. Because of this, and because the length of their messages was restricted to the size of a computerized message, it was ensured that the information value of the messages of both computerized coaches and human coaches was similar. Each coach was paired with one coachee from condition 1 and one from condition 2. Coachees received two messages per week for three weeks (after one initial week of monitoring), so each coach was asked to write a total of four messages per week. The coaches received automated requests by email to write their coaching messages in the online form. Coach compliance was very high: of the 240 messages in total, only 3 were missed. Coachees in all conditions received their coaching messages at the same time.

Procedure for Coachees. Coachees were divided into the different experimental conditions (1,2,3,4) in order of admission. Depending on the condition, coachees were told either that they were being paired with a human coach or with eMate. It was explained that after one week a goal would be set for them that would be based on the data from the first week. They would then receive coaching for a period of three weeks to reach that goal. The coachees were then asked to fill out the intake questionnaire on site. Coachees were asked to tap the widget every time they climbed a flight of stairs. In case no data was registered for a full day, the system automatically posed a question via the app about the (estimated) number of stairs taken during the previous day.

5   Results

For the analyses, three sets of data were considered. Dataset A (N=74) groups coachees based on the experimental condition that they were assigned to (1 to 4). It excludes coachees who failed to fill out the final questionnaire. Dataset A is used for all analyses concerned with differences in the entire group before and after the coaching interventions. Dataset B (N=64) was prepared by taking the coachees' reported belief about their coach into account. Someone who was assigned to condition 1 but reported a belief that his or her coach was a computer, was for all practical purposes in a similar state as coachees in condition 2 (recall Fig. 3). Because the study focuses on the effects of the belief about one's coach, a number of people were regrouped based on their reported beliefs (see the following subsection). In addition, coachees who reported to have no idea whether they were coached by a person or a computer were removed. Dataset B is used for analyses about differences between coachees in the different conditions. Finally, dataset C (N=60) comprises all coachees for whom data was collected from the stair climbing widget. People who stopped before the end of the experiment (5 people) and those who didn't regularly use the widget (7 people) were excluded. The grouping of coachees from dataset B is also used in dataset C (i.e., the condition is determined by the reported belief). Dataset C is used for analyzing the reported stair usage data collected via the widget.

Beliefs about Coaches: The Success of the Deception. For the experiment to yield valid results, it was crucial to establish that the deception was successful. To check this, coachees were asked in the evaluation survey whether they thought they were being coached by eMate or by a human coach. The data shows that in the deception conditions (2 and 3), only 3 people were not fooled (14.29%; in condition 3).[3] A number of people were unsure or just did not remember. This happened almost equally often in the 4 conditions. Given that the number of skeptical people in condition 1 was equal to that of condition 3, there are no indications that coachees in one of the deception conditions were aware of the deception. We therefore conclude that the deception was successful.

Effectiveness of the Intervention. An important outcome measure of the study was the relative effect of the intervention.[4] Our hypothesis was that the belief coachees have about the identity of their coach (human or computer) will have no effect on effectiveness. Moreover, we expected the intervention to have a positive effect on the number of stairs that coachees climbed.

To analyze the effect of the intervention, we used the data that was collected by the widget (dataset C). The widget data, combined with the estimates that participants provided the following day if they had forgotten to register their stairs use, resulted in a fairly complete set of data of the number of stairs taken each day. The number of

---

[3] To construct dataset B, these 3 people from condition 3 — who rightly believed they were being coached by eMate — were placed in condition 4. In addition, the 4 coachees who believed that they had a computerized coach in condition 1 were placed in condition 2.

[4] Because there was no control group, no conclusions can be drawn about the effectiveness of the intervention itself.

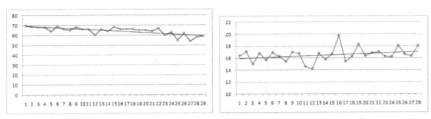

(a) Number of users using the widget per day. (b) Average number of stairs climbed per day for the total sample.

Fig. 5. Widget data

active users per day (those who registered at least 1 stairs event) only slightly decreased during the course of the experiment (from 69 to 59) as can be seen in Fig. 5a. To be able to compare the effects in the different groups, we examined the effect on the total sample. A graphical representation of the average numbers of stairs climbed per day is presented in Fig. 5b. A slight increase during the intervention is visible.

We define the effectiveness as the increase in the number of stairs climbed in the last week compared with the first week. The mean number of stairs taken for the total sample is 16.29 (SD=8.31) in the first week and 16.80 (SD=8.87) in the last. This difference is not significant (paired t-test, p=0.69).

The mean number of stairs climbed in the first and last week of the experiment for all groups is listed in Table 2. Except for groups 3 and 5, all groups showed an increase. There is a visible difference between group 5 (belief human) and group 6 (belief computer), but it is not significant (t-test, p=0.36).

Table 2. Mean of stairs climbed

Group	Mean first week	Mean last week	Difference	N
1	19.05	**19.07**	+0.02	12
2	12.18	**13.71**	+1.53	16
3	18.50	17.53	-0.97	16
4	17.19	**18.87**	+1.68	16
5	18.73	18.19	-0.54	28
6	14.68	**16.29**	+1.61	32
7	15.12	**16.01**	+0.89	28
8	17.84	**18.20**	+0.36	32

The effectiveness of the intervention was also assessed by examining the answer given to the question in the surveys about the number of stairs taken per week. We found a slight, but non-significant increase in the mean for the total sample (of approx. 0.2 points, wilcoxon signed rank test). There were no significant differences for any of the groups.

In the evaluation survey coachees were asked to what extent they found the different aspects of the system motivating on a 5-point Likert scale. As can be seen in Table 6, the use of the widget was perceived as the most motivating aspect of the system (median answer: 'quite'), followed by the coaching messages from the app (median answer: 'somewhat'). There was no significant difference between groups in dataset A or B.

Effect Measure: Perceived Influence of the Intervention. Perceived influence was defined as the extent to which people found that the intervention contributed positively to their behavior. Our hypothesis was that there will be no difference in how influential people perceive the intervention to be. Of the 74 coachees who filled out the evaluation survey (dataset A), 37.8% thought the intervention did not have a positive impact on their behavior. 32.4% were ambivalent, and 29.7% thought they were influenced positively. For the analysis of this question, the Likert-like item was recoded to numerical values from 1-5, where a higher value represents a more positive answer. The mean answer for all coachees was 2.85 (SD=1.06). Table 3 shows the means for all groups in A and Table 4 shows the means of all groups in B. At face value, both tables suggest that

Table 3. Means perceived influence (A)

Group	Mean	SD	N
1	3	0.87	17
2	2.68	1.06	19
3	3.05	1.20	21
4	2.65	1.06	17
5	3.03	1.05	38
6	2.67	1.04	36
7	2.83	0.97	36
8	2.87	1.14	38

Table 4. Means perceived influence (B)

Group	Mean	SD	N
1	3.18	0.60	11
2	2.5	0.89	20
3	3.12	1.20	16
4	2.65	1.17	17
5	3.15	0.99	27
6	2.57	1.01	37
7	2.74	0.86	31
8	2.88	1.19	33

the people who believed that they were being coached by a human, gave slightly more positive answers (see groups 1, 3 and 5). A Wilcoxon rank sum test was performed on dataset B for groups 5 (N=27) and 6 (N=37). This showed a difference that was significant at the $p<0.05$ level (W = 648, p=0.036). This finding suggests that people who believe that their coach is human indeed report more positively about the influence of coaching. To rule out that this difference was related to a difference in backend, Wilcoxon rank sum tests were also performed on the subgroups of 5 and 6, namely 1 and 3, and 2 and 4, respectively. These tests did not yield any significant differences, which is evidence for homogeneity within groups 5 and 6.

Effect Measure: Stage of Change. We expected that in all conditions there would be an overall improvement in stage of change. We examined dataset A with respect to the stage of change questions from the survey. The results are in Table 5. After recoding the stages to numerical values (PC=1 and M=5) the average stage at the start of the experiment was 4.18 and at the end 4.37 (a non-significant increase of 0.19). There was no significant difference in the pattern of change between the experimental groups (1-4 and 5-8). Two observations can be made from Table 5. First, the vast majority of the coachees started out and ended up in the Maintenance stage (72% and 78%, respectively). In stage M participants could not improve, and in stage A participants could only progress to M when they performed the behavior for six consecutive months, which was longer than the duration of the study. As such, only 21 people could improve their stage. Second, the overall trend is that people move from stages of non-compliance (PC,C and P) to stages of compliance (A and M). As part of the analysis described in [11], it was examined whether participants who could improve their adherence, did indeed improve. The results show that participants who started in stage PC, P or C (N=18) improved significantly over the course of the study (Wilcoxon signed rank test, p<0.01). On average they improved one stage. Those who started out in A and M did not change significantly.

Effect Measure: Trust. We also examined the influence of the identity of the coach on trust. Our hypothesis was that the belief coachees have about the identity of their coach (human or computer) will have no effect on trust. To test this, we analyzed the survey answers from the HCT scale [15]. The subscales of reliability, competence, understanding, faith and attachment were analyzed, as well as the individual items (5 questions per subscale). The answers to the questions were on a 5-point Likert scale and were recoded to values from 1 to 5 (3 = 'don't agree, don't disagree'). The means of all answers are shown in Table 7. In dataset A we found that the overall trust value for the system is average (3.02). The values for the subscales faith and attachment have the lowest means (2.73 and 2.60, respectively), while the subscale understanding had the highest mean (3.69). For checking for differences between groups, dataset B was used. None of the subscales of trust showed a statistical difference between the groups (t-test).

6   Discussion

Both the analyses of the widget data and of the survey data concerning the stage of change showed no effect from the coachee's belief about coach identity on the effectiveness of the interventions. This confirms hypothesis 1. Although overall the coachees improved — both with respect to the widget data and their stage of change — these improvements were non-significant for the total group of coachees. However, it should be mentioned that the questions in the survey might be too coarse-grained to report small differences, as the scale increments by 10 stairs.

Contrary to hypothesis 2, coachees judged the intervention to have more positive influence if they believed to be coached by a human coach. Considering that our analysis of trust showed no difference in trust between groups, confirming hypothesis 3, it might

Table 5. Transitions in stages of change

stage of change	start number	end number	change
Precontemplation (PC)	6	7	+1
Contemplation (C)	10	5	-5
Planning (P)	2	0	-2
Action (A)	3	4	+1
Maintenance (M)	53	58	+5

Table 6. Motivational aspects

Scale item	Mean	SD
coach messages on app	2.11	0.96
questions on app	1.99	0.92
use of widget	3.32	0.97
use of website	1.73	0.87
participation of others	1.97	1.13
total motivating aspects	2.22	0.57

Table 7. HCT scale means

Scale	Mean	SD
reliability	3.05	0.67
competence	3.03	0.66
understanding	3.69	0.69
faith	2.73	0.65
attachment	2.60	0.77
total HCT	3.02	0.48

be that people are more familiar with humans than computers in a coaching role, and that this shapes their evaluation of the system. Additional work is needed to support this hypothesis. Alternatively, there might have been a general skepticism about the extent of human involvement, as the questions that all coachees received were repetitive and obviously (and transparently) computer-generated. While this aspect of the experiment had been explained to the coachees, it might have contributed to some people's skepticism. Concerning the use of eMate, it can be concluded that overall the coachees felt that the system was averagely trustworthy. Their cognition-based trust was rated higher than their affect-based trust: coachees felt they had a good understanding of the system, but their attachment to the system and faith in its capabilities was somewhat lacking.

The results from this study provide initial insights into the social aspects of e-coaching. However, we acknowledge that the study has several limitations. First, the study covers only one sample of young, technology-savvy people. To draw general conclusions, a larger study with a wider set of coachees will have to be conducted. Second, it is possible that the application area plays a role in people's judgments about the trustworthiness of a system (i.e., it might be the case that it is easier to trust a system that stimulates exercise than one that supports medication intake). To investigate this, similar studies will have to be performed in different domains (preferably ones in which the stakes of change are different, such as for therapy adherence). Third, the method for measuring the number of stairs that people take can be improved. For future work, it would be beneficial to supplement or supplant the stair usage logging mechanism with accelerometer data. Fourth, most coachees were assigned the stage 'maintenance' based on their self-reports, which made it hard to improve their stage of change. One explanation is that all coachees already chose stairs over elevators, and needed little encouragement to take the stairs more often. Another possible explanation is that the questions used to determine the stage of change did not completely match the spectrum of the different stages. This explanation is given some weight by the fact that in the literature there is no standardized answer to the question of how people should be assigned to stages of change and which empirically validated surveys are most suitable (for discussion, see [24]). In future work an effort could be made to compare different surveys to determine people's stage of change.

7   Conclusion and Future Work

This paper has described a monthlong experiment of e-coaching in the wild: people received coaching outside of the lab for an activity with known health benefits. The coaching messages that coachees received were either computer-generated or written by a human being, but coachees were sometimes purposefully misled about the identity of their coach (human or computer). The results suggest that the belief that coachees had about the identity of their coach had no effect on the effectiveness of the coaching. Although research is needed to establish that this result holds in different domains, this is a first indication that e-coaching can be successful without the (transparent) involvement of a human coach. Second, the data suggests that people do have a bias towards human coaching with regard to judging how much positive influence coaching has on their behavior. Lastly, people showed no difference in trust towards human coaches or computerized coaches. Overall, people judged both types of coaches as averagely trustworthy. This is a noteworthy finding, as trust is the key ingredient of successful coach-coachee relationships [9]. Moreover, this judgement appears to be further evidence that, at least with regard to trust, people do treat computers as social actors.

Acknowledgments. This research was supported by Philips and Technology Foundation STW, Nationaal Initiatief Hersenen en Cognitie NIHC under the Partnership programme Healthy Lifestyle Solutions. We thank Inge Wolsky for her contributions to the content of the messages.

References

[1] Anderson, J.H., Kamphorst, B.A.: Ethics of e-coaching: Implications of employing pervasive computing to promote healthy and sustainable lifestyles. In: Proc. of IEEE SIPC Workshop 2014, in Conjunction with PerCom 2014, pp. 351–356. IEEE (2014)

[2] Bandura, A.: Guide for constructing self-efficacy scales. In: Pajares, F., Urdan, T. (eds.) Self-efficacy Beliefs of Adolescents, pp. 307–337. Adolescence and Education, Information Age Publishing (2006)

[3] Bickmore, T.W., Picard, R.W.: Establishing and maintaining long-term human-computer relationships. ACM Transactions of Computer-Human Interaction 12(2), 293–327 (2005)

[4] Blount, S.: When social outcomes aren't fair. Organizational Behavior and Human Decision Processes 63(2), 131–144 (1995)

[5] Bode, C., Thoolen, B.J., de Ridder, D.T.D.: Het meten van proactieve copingvaardigheden. Psychometrische eigenschappen van de utrechtse proactieve coping competentie lijst (UPCC). Psychologie & Gezondheid 36, 81–91 (2008)

[6] Endler, N., Parker, D.: Coping Inventory for Stressful Situations (CISS): Manual. Multi Health Systems, Toronto (1999) (Dutch translation by De Ridder, D.T.D., Maes, S.)

[7] Fogg, B.J.: Persuasive Technology: Using computers to change what we think and do. Morgan Kaufmann Publishers, San Francisco (2003)

[8] Fogg, B.J., Nass, C.: Silicon sycophants: The effects of computers that flatter. International Journal of Human-Computer Studies 46(5), 551–561 (1997)

[9] Gyllensten, K., Palmer, S.: The coaching relationship: An interpretative phenomenological analysis. International Coaching Psychology Review 2(2), 168–177 (2007)

[10] Kamphorst, B.A., Kalis, A.: Why option generation matters for the design of autonomous e-coaching systems. AI & Society (2014) (online)

[11] Kamphorst, B.A., Klein, M.C.A., Van Wissen, A.: Autonomous e-coaching in the wild: Empirical validation of a model-based reasoning system. In: Proceedings of the 13th International Conference on Autonomous Agents and Multiagent Systems (AAMAS 2014), pp. 725–732. ACM, New York (2014)

[12] Klein, M., Mogles, N., van Wissen, A.: Why won't you do what's good for you? Using intelligent support for behavior change. In: Salah, A.A., Lepri, B. (eds.) HBU 2011. LNCS, vol. 7065, pp. 104–115. Springer, Heidelberg (2011)

[13] Klein, M.C.A., Mogles, N.M., Van Wissen, A.: An intelligent coaching system for therapy adherence. IEEE Pervasive Computing 12(3), 22–30 (2013)

[14] Lee, J.R., Nass, C.I.: Trust in computers: The computers-are-social-actors (CASA) paradigm and trustworthiness perception in human-computer communication. In: Latusek, D., Gerbasi, A. (eds.) Trust and Technology in a Ubiquitous Modern Environment: Theoretical and Methodological Perspectives, pp. 1–15. IGI Global (2010)

[15] Madsen, M., Gregor, S.: Measuring human-computer trust. In: Proc. of the 11th Australian Conference on Information Systems, pp. 6–8 (2000)

[16] McAuley, E., Courneya, K.S.: The subjective exercise experiences scale (SEES): Development and preliminary validation. Journal of Sport and Exercise Psychology 16(2), 163–177 (1994)

[17] Nass, C., Moon, Y., Carney, P.: Are people polite to computers? Responses to computer-based interviewing systems. Journal of Applied Social Psychology 29(5), 1093–1110 (1999)

[18] Prochaska, J., DiClemente, C.: The transtheoretical approach: Crossing traditional boundaries of therapy. Dow Jones-Irwin, Homewood (1984)

[19] Pruitt, D.G., Carnevale, P.J.: Negotiation in social conflict. Thomson Brooks/Cole Publishing Co., Belmont (1993)

[20] Reed, G.R., Velicer, W.F., Prochaska, J.O., Rossi, J.S., Marcus, B.H.: What makes a good staging algorithm: Examples from regular exercise. American Journal of Health Promotion 12(1), 57–66 (1997)

[21] Reeves, B., Nass, C.: The Media Equation: How People Treat Computers, Television, and New Media Like Real People and Places. CSLI Lecture Notes Series, vol. 63, Center for the Study of Language and Informatics (1996)

[22] Ryan, R.M., Connell, J.P.: Perceived locus of causality and internalization: Examining reasons for acting in two domains. Journal of Personality and Social Psychology 57(5), 749–761 (1989)

[23] Sorbi, M.J., Mak, S.B., Houtveen, J.H., Kleiboer, A.M., Van Doornen, L.J.P.: Mobile web-based monitoring and coaching: Feasibility in chronic migraine. Journal of Medical Internet Research 9(5) (2007)

[24] Sutton, S.: Back to the drawing board? A review of applications of the transtheoretical model to substance use. Addiction 96(1), 175–186 (2001)

[25] Van Dongen, K., Van Maanen, P.P.: Under-reliance on the decision aid: A difference in calibration and attribution between self and aid. In: Proc. of the Human Factors and Ergonomics Society's 50th Annual Meeting, San Francisco, CA, vol. 50, pp. 225–229 (2006)

[26] Van Wissen, A., Gal, Y., Kamphorst, B.A., Dignum, M.V.: Human-agent teamwork in dynamic environments. Computers in Human Behavior 28(1), 23–33 (2012)

[27] Van Wissen, A., Van Diggelen, J., Dignum, V.: The effects of cooperative agent behavior on human cooperativeness. In: Proc. of AAMAS, pp. 1179–1180 (2009)

[28] Warner, T.: E-coaching systems: Convenient, anytime, anywhere, and nonhuman. Performance Improvement 51(9), 22–28 (2012)

Just the Way You Chat: Linking Personality, Style and Recognizability in Chats

Giorgio Roffo[1], Cinzia Giorgetta[2], Roberta Ferrario[2], and Marco Cristani[1]

[1] Università degli Studi di Verona, Strada Le Grazie 15, I-37134 Verona, Italy
[2] ISTC–CNR, via alla Cascata 56/C, I-38123 Povo (Trento), Italy

Abstract. Text chatting represents a hybrid type of communication, where textual information is delivered following turn-taking dynamics, which characterize spoken interactions. It is interesting to understand whether special interactional behavior can emerge in chats, similarly as it does in face-to-face exchanges. In this work, we focus on the writing style of individuals, analyzing how it can be recognized given a portion of chat, and how personality comes into play in this scenario. Two interesting facts do emerge: 1) some traits correlate significantly with some characteristics of people's chatting style, captured by stylometric features; 2) some of such features are very effective in recognizing a person among a gallery of diverse individuals. This seems to suggest that some personality traits could lead people to chat with a particular style, which turns out to be very recognizable. For example, motor impulsiveness gives a significative (negative) correlation with the use of the suspension points (. . .), that is also one of the most discriminative characteristics in chats. This and other relations emerge on a dataset on 45 subjects, monitored for 3 months, whose personality traits have been analyzed through self-administered questionnaires. What turns out is that chatting seems to be more than just typing.

Keywords: chat analysis, personality traits, authorship attribution.

1   Introduction

It is widely-known that written text (books, newspapers) conveys a great deal of information about the writer, relying on features that are not exhausted by those connected to semantic content; personality and identity traits can be inferred from text, through computational approaches, with a high accuracy [1–5]. But "written text" is not only books and newspapers: with the diffusion of the Internet, new kinds of media have arisen, such as online texts and electronic messages. Among these new media, text chats represent a social phenomenon: in 2009, 47 billion of instant messages have been delivered on a daily basis, with 1 billion of users worldwide. Under the perspective of pragmatics and social signal processing, chats are intriguing entities, representing crossbreeds of literary text and spoken conversations, due to the turn-taking dynamics with which text is delivered. In this respect, it is interesting to verify the presence of nonverbal cues

H.S. Park et al. (Eds.): HBU 2014, LNCS 8749, pp. 30–41, 2014.

in chats. Nonverbal signals enrich the spoken conversation by characterizing how sentences are uttered by a speaker [6], forging a unique style that characterizes the latter among many other subjects. In the same vein, they express personal beliefs, thoughts, emotions and personality. In this work we analyze how these insights may be applied to text chats, extracting features dubbed as "stylometric", since they codify the style of an author. Recently, specific features have been shown to finely recognize an author through his/her style. In this paper, we continue the work, checking whether style is effectively linked with the personality or other psychological or interactional traits of the speaker; this allows to close the loop, exploring how personality can make speakers recognizable by the uniqueness of their style.

To this sake, we consider a novel dataset of chats in italian language. The dataset contains data on 45 subjects, related to their chatting activity with single individuals for a time lapse of three months on average. In order to analyze the chatting style of a subject, we take into consideration 20 hybrid stylometric features recently proposed in [7]; to gather information on the personal characteristics of each individual, we use two well-known self-administered questionnaires, the former focused on 3 different impulsiveness factors (attentional, motor and non-planning impulsiveness), and the latter on 4 different psychological factors involved in human interactions (ability on taking others' perspective, empathic concern, fantasy scale and personal distress in interpersonal settings).

Two interesting results emerge: first, 5 psychological factors seem to correlate with 7 out of 20 stylometric features, in a statistically significant way (p-$value <$ 0.05); for example, our data showed that subjects with higher lack of attention and cognitive instability were slower in providing their answers.

The second result follows by applying person recognition using stylometric features. The idea is to take a portion of a chat (10 turns of an individual) and to guess his/her identity, comparing against a gallery of 45 individuals. For this sake, we analyze each feature independently, capturing their appropriateness in distinguishing one subject from the other. Thus, we can single out highly expressive features (capable of recognizing a person with some accuracy) which are possibly correlated with a given personality trait expressed by a psychological factor. These findings seem to suggest that there are some personality traits that lead people to chat with a particular style, which turns out to be very recognizable. For example, the use of the suspension points (...) is a discriminative characteristic in chats, and shows a significant (negative) correlation with motor impulsiveness (the tendency to act on the spur of the moment).

The rest of the paper is organized as follows: in Section 2 we present the literature review, focusing on the computational approaches of chat analysis. In Section 3 we present our dataset, illustrating our analysis. In the same section our novel stylometric features are presented and the results of correlation between personality traits and stylometric features are reported in Section 3.3, while the results on identity recognition are presented in Section 3.4. Finally, conclusions and future perspectives are presented in Section 4.

2   Related Work

Although some computational approaches that try to infer personality traits from text are present in the literature, all these are focused on a semantic analysis of the content [2, 8]; on the contrary, in this work a semantic analysis of the text is, for privacy issues, absent. More importantly, none of the mentioned approaches have been applied to chats. Concerning the author recognition issue, the most related field of studies is that of Authorship Attribution (AA), that has as main aim to automatically recognize the author of a given text sample, based on the analysis of *stylometric* cues (see Table 1).

Typically, state-of-the-art approaches extract stylometric features from data and use discriminative classifiers to identify the author (each author corresponds to a class). The application of AA to chat conversations is recent (see [4] for a survey), with [1, 5, 9] the most cited works. In [5], a framework for authorship attribution of online messages has been developed to address the identity-tracing problem. Stylometric features were fed into SVM and neural networks on 20 subjects, validating the recognition accuracy on 30 random messages. PCA-like projection has been applied in [1] for authorship identification and similarity detection on 100 potential authors of e-mails, instant messages, feedback comments and program code. A unified data mining approach has been presented in [10] to address the challenges of authorship attribution in anonymous online textual communication (email, blog, IM) for the purpose of cybercrime investigation.

In the last ten years, authorship attribution and forensic analysis have extended their research to IM communication [11]. In [3], 4 authors of IM conversations have been identified based on the sentence structure and their use of special characters, emoticons, and abbreviations. Most recently, ad-hoc features for analyzing chats and perform author identification and verification have been presented in [7], dubbed as *turn-taking based* features (see Table 1).

In our work, we examine chats among pairs of people. These conversations can be considered as sequences of *turns*, where each *turn* is a set of symbols consecutively typed by one subject without being interrupted by the other person. Each conversation ends when no turn does occur for at least 30 minutes. In addition, each turn is composed by one or more *sentences*: a sentence is a stream of symbols which is ended by a "return" character. Each sentence is labeled by a temporal ID, reporting the time of delivery.

In the study each character constituting a word has been substituted by an X symbol, so that the content of the conversation is disregarded, but other features, such as length of words, punctuation, emoticons etc. are preserved and analyzed. Other elements that are left opaque are the relationship the speakers entertain with their interlocutors and the psychological character of the latter. Nonetheless, independently from this, we are able to re-identify the speaker(s) through their chat style.

Table 1. Synopsis of the 20 features used in our work. In squared parenthesis, the numeric range of values taken by each feature in this dataset.

Group	Subgroup	*Name*, description and [range]	References
Lexical	Word level	**#Words** (=W): number of words per turn - [0,253]; **Avg. word length**: average word length in a turn - [0,443]	[1, 3–5, 10]
	Character level	**#Chars** (=C): number of characters in a turn - [0,1624]; **#Uppercase letters**: number of uppercase characters - [0,05]; **#Uppercase/C**: number of uppercase characters divided by C - [0,1]	[1, 3–5]
Syntactic	Punctuation	**# ? and ! marks**: number of question and exclamation marks summed together, in a turn - [0,4]; **#Three points (...)**: number of occurrences of three points (...) in a turn - [0,15]; **#Marks (",.:*;)**: number of marks (",.:*;) in a turn - [0,119]	[1, 3–5, 10]
	Emoticons	**#Emoticons**: total number of Skype emoticons in a turn - [0,16]; **#Emoticons/C**: number of emoticons divided by C - [0,1]; **# emoticons/W**: number of emoticons divided by W - [0,4]; emoticons categories such as **#Pos. emo.**, that counts the occurrences of happiness, love, intimacy, etc. icons (20 emot. types in total) - [0,4]; **#Neg. emo.**: address fear, anger, etc. (19 emot. types in total) - [0,3]; and **#Oth. emo.**, neutral emoticons portray actions, objects etc. (62 emot. types in total) - [0,16]	[3, 4, 7]
Turn-taking	Temporal (in seconds)	**Turn duration**: time spent to complete a turn - [0,1800]; **Answer time**: time spent to answer a question expressed in the previous turn of the other interlocutor - [0, 1784]	[7]
	Tempo/lexical	**Char/Word writing speed**: number of typed characters or words per second - [0,350] and [0,67];	[7]
	Lexical	**Imitation rate/C, Imitation rate/W**: ratio between number of chars -or words- in current turn and number of chars -or words- in previous turn of the interlocutor - [0,1] and [0,1]	[7]

From each turn, all stylometric features are extracted, generating a number each; therefore, for each conversation, we obtain T feature values. The description of the employed features is presented in Tab. 1: for the sake of brevity, we did an initial feature selection, pruning away features producing less than 50% of nAUC (see next), coming out with 20 cues left. The features are nonverbal, that is, they ignore the content of the chat; in this sense, they are comparable to nonverbal signals in spoken conversation (nodding, speaking louder etc.).

3   Our Analysis

In this section we illustrate our analysis, discussing the results.

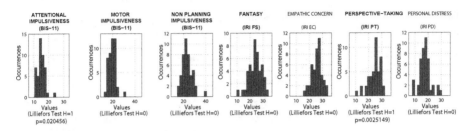

Fig. 1. Traits distribution. On the bottom, the output of the Lilliefors test for distribution normality. In bold, those personality traits which correlate with at least one stylometric feature.

3.1   The Dataset

Our dataset focuses on 45 subjects[1] (Master and PhD students, Post-doc associates and various professionals; 29 male, 16 female; average age: 30,25 years), involved in dyadic, spontaneous conversations; moreover, the chats have been performed before the beginning of the study, when the subjects were not aware that they would have been used for such purpose. This ensures that the behavior of the subjects is natural and no attempt has been made to modify the style in any sense. From the raw conversations, we extract the features discussed above. The number of turns per subject ranges between 20 and 100. Concerning the personality traits, participants were asked to fill the following two well-known self-administered questionnaires, aimed at evaluating psychological factors:

1. The Barratt Impulsiveness Scale, version 11 (Bis-11) [13], to measure the levels of impulsiveness, based on three different sub-scales: "attentional impulsiveness", indicating a lack of attention and cognitive instability, "motor impulsiveness", indicating a lack of control in motor behavior, and "non-planning impulsiveness", indicating a deficit in planning their own behavior. The total number of items is 30, answered on a 4-points scale, ranging from 'never' to 'always'.

2. Interpersonal Reactivity Index (IRI) [14], to test their ability to take others' perspective (PT) and empathic concerns (EC), to get caught up in fictional stories and imagine oneself in the same situations as fictional characters (FS), and finally to test their "self-oriented" feelings of personal anxiety in interpersonal settings (PD). This questionnaire presents 28 items answered on a 5-point Likert scale, ranging from 'does not describe me well' to 'describes me very well'.

In Fig. 1, we report the traits statistics.

---

[1] The number of participants in these experiments is relatively small, and this can be seen as a limitation, as it may partially restrict the generalization of the results. However, the present study is in line with the sample size of other studies in the psychological field, wherein, in within-subjects design, the number of participants is typically between 20 (e.g., for studies in neuroscience field) and 40 (e.g., for behavioral studies). Also, in other more related studies, such as [12], in which the role of personality traits in human-robot vs. human-human interaction has been investigated, the sample size is even lower ($N = 28$).

3.2   The Stylometric Features

Thanks to our framework, we were able to design a set of stylometric features which follow the idea of [7], that is, of using the turn length, and not simply the entire conversation, as fundamental entity for computing stylometric statistics.

We have paid much attention to privacy issues: the idea is to neglect the content of the conversation, accounting only for the way in which it is performed. Our features follow this guideline, avoiding any kind of natural language processing, while other features, as length of words, punctuation, emoticons etc. are preserved and analyzed.

For each person involved in a conversation, we analyze his/her stream of turns (suppose T), ignoring the semantic input from the other subject. This means that we assume that the chat style (as modeled by our features) is invariant through different interlocutors, with whom the subject entertain different kinds of relationships.

From each turn, a stylometric feature is extracted, generating a number; therefore, with T turns we obtain T feature values. Depending on the kind of feature and task to perform (measuring correlations or doing person identification), an histogram or the mean/median is computed, and the resulting measure becomes a part of the signature which characterizes a given individual. In the following, the list of the features together with their explanation is presented.

For the sake of clarity, our features will be presented following the taxonomy analyzed in the state of the art (see Tab. 1). For convenience, and whereas possible, we have kept the name of the features proposed in the literature.

How the features have been treated to calculate correlations with personality traits or similarities enabling recognition, will be discussed in the following. In the list below, the numbers in parenthesis indicate the feature ID.

Lexical Features

(1) **Number of words (#Words)**: number of words per turn. With "word" we intend a string of *characters* (see below);

(2) **Number of chars (#Chars)**: number of characters per turn. With "character", we intend every normal key on the XXX keyboard[2], ignoring special keys like the SPACE, CTRL, etc.;

(3) **Number of uppercase chars (#Uppercase Letters)**: number of uppercase characters in a turn;

(4) **Number of uppercase chars / number of chars (#Uppercase/#C)**: usually, entire words written in capital letters indicate a strong emotional message. This feature accounts for such communicative tendency;

(5) **Mean word length (Avg. word length)**: average length of the words in a turn;

(6-7) **1(2)-order length transitions (1oLT, 2oLT)**: these features resemble the n-grams of [1]; the strong difference here is in the fact that we consider

---

[2] The kind of keyboard has been removed for anonymity reasons.

solely the length of the words, and not their content. In practice, for a noLT of order $n = 1$ (1oLT), we build counting matrices that in the entry i, j, $1 \leq i, j \leq I$, exhibit the number of times we move from a word of length i to a word of length j. The count matrices are then normalized, so that they can be seen as transition matrices of a Markov chain. In our case, we set $I = 15$. 2oLT are modeled by 3D transition matrices of size $I \times I \times I$. We do not take into account superior orders, for sparsity issues (the resulting hypervolumes will have many entries at 0). These features are collected over whole conversations, rather than on single turns.

Syntactic Features

(8) **Number of ? and ! marks (#? & ! marks):** we keep the "?" and the "!" marks in the same feature, since taken separately their relevance is very low. In practice this feature highlights the fact that a conversation is lively and conveys a great deal of (positive or negative) emotions. It also shows the will of the subject of generating a reaction in the interlocutor;

(9) **Number of suspension points (#Three points (...)):** this feature may show the uncertainty of the subject with respect to the sentence just written, or it may suggest to the interlocutor some unspoken consequent of what has been declared explicitly in the previous sentence;

(10) **Number of generic marks (#Marks (",.:*;)):** a high number of generic marks (",.:*;) usually indicates a more accurate writing style. In particular, they are mostly used to give structure to the sentences and articulate a discourse. This can either be a peculiar characteristic of the subject, or it may hint to the fact that the subject is very determined with respect to what he/she is saying and thus provides it with a structure to make explicit that it is the result of an elaborated thought;

(11,12,13) **Number of *positive, negative* and *uncategorized* emoticons (Pos. emo, Neg. emo, Oth. emo**, respectively): features related to emoticons aim at individuating a particular mood expressed in a turn. In particular, 101 diverse emoticons have been divided in three classes, portraying positive emotions (happiness, love, intimacy, etc. − 20 emot.), negative emotions (fear, anger, etc. − 19 emot.) and other emoticons (portraying actions, objects etc. − 62 emot.);

(14) **Number of emoticons (#Emoticons):** Number of emoticons in a turn, independently from their type;

(15-16) **Number of emoticons / number of words (chars) (#Emoticons/#W, #Emoticons/#C**, respectively): it considers how often we inject pictorial symbols in a sentence considering the number of words (chars) typed; it measures how much the subject willingly shows his/her emotions, attitudes, intended humor etc.

Turn-taking Features

(17) **Turn duration**: We indicate with T the length of the period in which a turn is kept (before pressing the "return" key);

(18-19) **Word writing speed**: it measures the turn duration divided by the number $\#Words$ or $\#Chars$ of written words/chars in a turn;

(20-21) **Imitation per word, per char (Imitation rate / W, Imitation rate / C)**: ratio between number of chars -or words- in the current turn and number of chars -or words- in the previous turn of the interlocutor; this feature models the tendency of a subject to imitate the conversation style of the interlocutor (at least for what concerns the length of the turns). The imitation feature accounts for some interactional attitudes of the subjects;

(22) **Answer time**: this feature is the time spent to answer a question presented in the previous turn of the interlocutor. We assume the presence of a question whenever there is a question mark.

Since these features are collected for each turn (except the 1oLT and 2oLT features), and assuming there are T turns in a conversation, we end up with T numbers for each feature.

These features were subsequently used for two applications: correlation with psychological traits and subject recognition. Depending on the task at hand, the feature values have been treated differently, as discussed in the following.

3.3   Correlations between Traits and Features

In order to discover a connection between psychological traits and features, we calculate the Pearson correlation coefficient (whereas both the distribution of features values and traits were normal), the Spearman coefficient otherwise. The test for normality is the Lilliefors test. Results are shown in Table 2, showing 7 significant correlations (p-value< 0.05)[3].

Our findings seem to suggest that subjects who score higher in attentional impulsiveness, then with higher lack of attention and cognitive instability, are also slower in providing answers to their partners, whereas those higher in motor impulsiveness use a lower number of suspension points, indicating they are loosing less time (before making a question or providing an answer) to think about what they have to write. Also, subjects with deficit in planning their own behavior (non-planning impulsiveness) seem to use a lower number of emoticons expressing positive emotions. In the same direction, those higher in attentional impulsiveness seem to use a higher number of emoticons expressing negative emotions. Relatively to traits involved in interpersonal interactions, our data show that subjects higher in fantasy scale (FS) seem to spend less time in typing words and single letters, showing they are faster in imaging what they can

---

[3] Although the r values of these correlations are around .30, and thus indicating a not really strong correlation, these also show a p value which is lower than .05 and thus significant and worth to be taken into consideration.

Table 2. Correlations between psychological traits and stylometric features. In parenthesis, the nAUC score, witnessing how effective is the feature in distinguishing people (the higher the more effective, see Section 3.4). Numerical values in the table indicate statistically significant correlations (*p-value*< 0.05).

	Attentional impulsiveness	Motor impulsiveness	Non planning	Fantasy scale	Perspective taking
#Three points (...) *(57.5)*	/	-0.32	/	/	/
#Uppercase/C *(59.3)*	/	/	/	-0.32	-0.35
Word writing speed *(61.3)*	/	/	/	-0.33	/
Char writing speed *(63.3)*	/	/	/	-0.32	/
Answer time *(51.2)*	0.30	/	/	/	/
#Pos. Emo. *(62)*	/	/	-0.29	/	/
#Neg. Emo. *(54.5)*	0.33	/	/	/	/

write and then in doing that. Instead, subjects with lower scores in FS, as well as those with lower ability in taking others' perspective (PT), seem to use a higher number of upper cases, as if they need to outline what they are writing.

3.4 The Recognition Approach

At this point, we want to understand the appropriateness of stylometric features in the task of recognizing a person given a portion of his/her chat. Let us suppose to have collected the features related to the conversations for two subjects, A and B (one conversation each). We now have to exploit them for obtaining a single distance, describing the overall similarity between A and B. As a first step, we derive a plausible distance for each feature separately: since we want to extract as much information as possible from the conversation, given T values of a feature, we organize them into an 8-bin histogram, where the range of the quantization values has been fixed by considering all the samples of the gallery. To match the two conversations, we thus employ the Bhattacharyya distance. The turns of each subject are split into *probe* and *gallery* set, where the probe samples serve as test, and are given to the recognizer, which evaluates the matches with the gallery elements. Probe and gallery set include 10 turns each: in this way, any bias due to differences in the amount of available material should be avoided. When possible, we pick different turns selections (maintaining their chronological order) in order to generate different probe/gallery partitions. In this sense, for each feature we repeat the re-identification 30 times, varying probe and gallery partitions. A particular feature of a single subject is extracted from the probe set, and matched against the corresponding gallery of features of all subjects. This happens for all the N subjects, resulting in a $N \times N$ distance matrix. Ranking in ascending order the N distances for each probe element allows one to compute the *Cumulative Match Characteristic* (CMC) curve, i.e., the expectation of finding the correct match in the top n positions of the ranking. The CMC is an effective performance measure for authorship attribution approaches [15], and in our case is a valid measure for evaluating the task of *identity recognition*: given a test sample, we want to discover the identity among a set of N subjects. In particular, the value

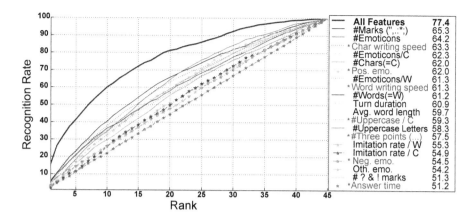

Fig. 2. CMC curves for each feature. After each feature, the value of the correspondent nAUC. With an asterisk, in red, we specify those features which correlate at least with a personality trait. The *All features* CMC indicates the performance of averaging the distance of all the features and calculating the ranking.

of the CMC curve at position 1 is the probability that the probe ID signature of a subject is closer to the gallery ID signature of the same subject than to any other gallery ID signature; the value of the CMC curve at position n is the probability of finding the correct match in the first n ranked positions.

Given the CMC curve for each feature (obtained by averaging on 30 trials), the normalized Area Under Curve (nAUC) is calculated as a measure of accuracy. The results are shown in Fig. 2, where the features are listed in decreasing order of accuracy. In red are portrayed those cues which correlate with at least one feature: for the sake of clarity, the nAUC value is reported also in Table 2. The Table seems to suggest an important fact: fantasy scale is the trait which is tightly related with the style of a person, making it very recognizable, since it affects the speed with which a person writes, and his/her usage of the uppercase letters. Once again, these data confirm that people with a higher ability in being caught up in fictional stories and in imaging themselves in the same situations of fictional characters are faster in imaging and then writing what they can say or answer to the person they are communicating with.

Another interesting observation can be assessed by looking at Fig. 2; all the CMC curves related to the different features are similar in expressivity, but not strongly effective; the probability of guessing the right people with only one attempt (corresponding to analyzing the performance of the CMC curve at rank 1) is below the 10%. Anyway, if we combine all features, mediating the related distances computed among the probe and the gallery subject, we obtain a much more informative curve (see Fig. 2, *All features*). In this case, getting the correct guess after the first attempt is above the 10%, and with the 60% of probability we can individuate the correct subject among the first 10 ranked subjects. This witnesses that the features model diverse and complementary stylistic aspects of a chat text; viceversa, except the #Uppercase/C stylometric feature, each feature seems to be connected with only one factor related with personality traits investigated here. These findings are very interesting as, congruently with the aim of this study, they clearly suggest that specific psychological factors related with impulsivity and involved in human interaction can be predictive of peculiar writing styles people use in the chat text. Finally, despite the recognition scores may appear low, one has to keep in mind that they are related to a soft biometric trait, that is, taken without the explicit cohoperation of the user [16]. In such a scenario, recognition performances are much lower than (hard) biometric traits (iris, fingerprint), and in line with the results presented.

4   Conclusions

The present study suggests that chatting via text is a very rich form of conversation; contrarily to what assumed until few years ago [17], chats allow to exchange more than simply verbal information: in particular, we have analyzed 7 personality traits, showing a significant correlation of 5 of them with 7 stylometric features. At the same time, these stylometric features turn out to be very helpful in discriminating one subject from the others, considering re-identification metrics. Putting together these two facts, what seems to emerge is that there are personality traits that could lead one to chat in a particular manner, which turns out to be very recognizable. This study constitutes an encouragement in pursuing this research direction, and should be considered a exploratory attempt, since many are the necessary improvements. First of all, the dataset should be enlarged for a more robust statistics support. Therefore, regression approaches will be needed for predicting the personality traits of an individual, given his/her chats. At the present moment, the data is not enough to support the training of a classifier, and the preliminary prediction results (done with Support Vector regression, under a Leave-One-Out cross-validation scheme) are not satisfactory. From a psychological perspective, a further step would be to investigate how these personality traits affect conversations in text chats focusing on more specific interactions, for example with co-workers, friends or unknown people. These specific interactions in particular can be decisive in determining whether it is possible to recognize the personality traits by written conversations, independently from the kind of relationships with the interlocutor and interactional setting. As for the application, this study paves the way for multimodal interfaces capable of recognizing the identity and/or the personality traits of a person, recommending for example specific typologies of interlocutors whom he/she would be more comfortable to talk with.

References

1. Abbasi, A., Chen, H., Nunamaker, J.F.: Stylometric identification in electronic markets: Scalability and robustness. Journal of Management Information Systems (JMIS) 25(1), 49–78 (2008)

2. Mairesse, F., Walker, M.A., Mehl, M.R., Moore, R.K.: Using linguistic cues for the automatic recognition of personality in conversation and text. Journal of Artificial Intelligence Research (JAIR) 30, 457–500 (2007)

3. Orebaugh, A., Allnutt, J.: Classification of instant messaging communications for forensics analysis. Social Networks, 22–28 (2009)

4. Stamatatos, E.: A survey of modern authorship attribution methods. Journal of the Association for Information Science and Technology (JASIST) 60(3), 538–556 (2009)

5. Zheng, R., Li, J., Chen, H., Huang, Z.: A framework for authorship identification of online messages: Writing-style features and classification techniques. Journal of the Association for Information Science and Technology (JASIST) 57(3), 378–393 (2006)

6. Knapp, M.L.: Nonverbal communication in human interaction, 8th edn., January 1. Cengage Learning (2013)

7. Roffo, G., Segalin, C., Vinciarelli, A., Murino, V., Cristani, M.: Reading between the turns: Statistical modeling for identity recognition and verification in chats. In: IEEE International Conference on Advanced Video and Signal-Based Surveillance, AVSS 2013 (2013)

8. Pennebaker, J.W., King, L.A.: Linguistic styles: language use as an individual difference. Journal of Personality and Social Psychology 77(6), 1296–1312 (1999)

9. Abbasi, A., Chen, H.: Writeprints: A stylometric approach to identity-level identification and similarity detection in cyberspace. ACM TOIS 26(2), 1–29 (2008)

10. Iqbal, F., Binsalleeh, H., Fung, B.C.M., Debbabi, M.: A unified data mining solution for authorship analysis in anonymous textual communications. Information Sciences (2011)

11. Gajadhar, J., Green, J.: Open Polytechnic of New Zealand, Open Polytechnic of New Zealand Staff. An Analysis of Nonverbal Communication in an Online Chat Group, Working papers, Open Polytechnic of New Zealand (2003)

12. Walters, M.L., Dautenhahn, K., Boekhorst, R., Koay, K.L., Kaouri, C., Woods, S., Nehaniv, C., Lee, D., Werry, I.: The influence of subjects' personality traits on personal spatial zones in a human-robot interaction experiment. In: International Workshop on Robot and Human Interactive Communication, RO-MAN 2005, August 13-15, pp. 347–352 (2005)

13. Patton, J.H., Stanford, M.S., Barratt, E.S.: Factor structure of the barratt impulsiveness scale. Journal of Clinical Psychology 51, 768–774 (1995)

14. Davis, M.H.: A multidimensional approach to individual differences in empathy. JSAS Catalog of Selected Documents in Psychology 10, 85–104 (1980)

15. Bolle, R., Connell, J., Pankanti, S., Ratha, N., Senior, A.: Guide to Biometrics. Springer (2003)

16. Dantcheva, A., Velardo, C., D'angelo, A., Dugelay, J.-L.: Bag of soft biometrics for person identification: New trends and challenges. Mutimedia Tools and Applications (October 2010)

17. Markey, P.M., Wells, S.M.: Interpersonal perception in internet chat rooms. Journal of Research in Personality 36(2), 134–146 (2002)

A New Multi-modal Dataset
for Human Affect Analysis

Haolin Wei[1], David S. Monaghan[1], Noel E. O'Connor[1], and Patricia Scanlon[2,*]

[1] Insight Centre for Data Analytics, Dublin City University, Ireland
[2] Bell Labs Ireland, Alcatel Lucent Dublin, Ireland

Abstract. In this paper we present a new multi-modal dataset of spontaneous three way human interactions. Participants were recorded in an unconstrained environment at various locations during a sequence of debates in a video conference, Skype style arrangement. An additional depth modality was introduced, which permitted the capture of 3D information in addition to the video and audio signals. The dataset consists of 16 participants and is subdivided into 6 unique sections. The dataset was manually annotated on a continuously scale across 5 different affective dimensions including arousal, valence, agreement, content and interest. The annotation was performed by three human annotators with the ensemble average calculated for use in the dataset. The corpus enables the analysis of human affect during conversations in a real life scenario. We first briefly reviewed the existing affect dataset and the methodologies related to affect dataset construction, then we detailed how our unique dataset was constructed.

Keywords: Spontaneous affect dataset, Continuous annotation, Multi-modal, Depth, Affect recognition.

1 Introduction

The interpretation of human affect plays an important role in our daily interactions, thus it is crucial for a computer to actually interpret these in order to develop a system that can engage a human in a smooth, natural and emotionally coloured way [1][2][3]. This requires rich sets of labelled [4] and application specific data with in a context that occurs naturally in daily-life [5][11].

There has been a growing interest in collecting multi-modal spontaneous affect datasets during last decade [3][4][12][13], however there is still a lack of emotionally rich social interactions that are captured in a natural real-life setting that is outside a laboratory environment. Such a dataset is required in order to develop affective analysis systems that can be used in daily life.

2D visual signals have been some of the most widely used modalities for affect recognition in the literature. Visual cues such as facial expressions and body gestures have been well studied [9][10][7]. However these 2D visual cues are highly

---

* This work was conducted whilst the author was with Bell Labs Ireland.

H.S. Park et al. (Eds.): HBU 2014, LNCS 8749, pp. 42–51, 2014.

sensitive to the capture environment such as illumination, occlusions and other changes in facial and body appearance such as glasses, mark-up, facial hair and clothes [6]. Moreover, the single 2D visual analysis is unable to fully capture the out-of-plane changes and structure information. For example certain facial actions such as Jaw Clench could be difficult to detect in a 2D view [6] and same body gesture could give different "appearance" when viewed in different perspectives [8]. In order to tackle these problems, 3D visual signals could be used. With the recent availability of affordable depth sensors (such as the Microsoft Kinect) offering easy access to 3D data of adequate quality, the depth modality has received a lot of attention as it can be used to improve the results and robustness of an affect recognition system. Bio signals such as eye gaze data, electrocardiogram (ECG), electrodermal activity (EDA), respiration amplitude, skin impedance and skin temperature have also been used for affect recognition. Although these modalities can be adapted when visual and audio modalities are not available, E.g. no visible face or speech production [12], they are usually perceived to be invasive and cumbersome and do not lend themselves to be utilised on a large scale basis [14].

In this paper we present one of the first spontaneous and continuous annotated multi-modal dataset focused on human interaction during a debate. The motivation behind building the dataset is driven by the development of a real-time automatic affect recognition system that could provide instant affective feedback to the users.

2   Related Work

As [4] suggested, in general, there are three types of interaction behaviour that have been used to capture human affect i) posed behaviour, where the participant is asked to perform a certain affective state such as happy, sad etc. ii) induced behaviour, where the participant is put in a controlled environment to elicit a certain affective state through various tasks such as watching movies or pictures. iii) spontaneous behaviour, which appear in real-life setting such as debates or other interactions that involve humans and/or machines. Among all three types of interaction scenarios, the posed affect is the easiest to design and capture. However, it have been proven that the affective state raised from a real-life context are more complex compare to the posed ones, as actors tend to exaggerate the affective state they are displaying [14]. Although the induced affective state could provide natural emotional response, it is usually not able to cover the full range and complex affective state as the interaction is restricted to a specific context [3][4]. Finally the spontaneous affect state is the hardest to capture as true affective state are relatively infrequent, short lived, and consist complex context-based changes [14]. Furthermore, by informing a participant that they are being recorded lead to a change in natural behaviours. However, by not informing participants that they are being recorded raises a myriad of ethical issues. In order to ethically capture the spontaneous affective state, various techniques have been developed: i) In [18] the author use a series of activities such as, listening to a joke or experiencing harsh insults from the experimenter to try to elicit target emotional state. ii) In [4] the authors use the survival task techniques where group discussion is promoted by asking participants to reach a consensus on how to survive in a disaster scenario.

Various multi-modal datasets that consist of spontaneous and socially enriched human affective states have been created in the last decade. The SE-MAINE [3] dataset was one of the first corpus focused on machine-human interaction using nonverbal expressions. It was released in 2007 and is one of the most widely used affect dataset for benchmarking human affect recognition systems [3][16][17]. It features continuous annotated audiovisual recordings of emotionally coloured conversations, elicited through a Sensitive Artificial Listener(SAL). There are four SALs where each SAL is designed to drive the user towards a specific affective state (angry, happy, gloomy and sensible) using predefined subscripts. The annotations include five core dimensions (valence, activation, power, anticipation/expectation) and optional descriptors such as basic emotions and epistemic states.

The Cam3D [13] corpus is a 3D multi-modal corpus which consists of elicited complex mental states. The dataset includes 12 mental states (thinking, concentrating, unsure, confused, triumphant, frustrated, angry, bored, neutral and surprised) which was captured using two High-definition (HD) cameras and two Kinect sensors. The community crowd-sourcing was used to annotate the data.

The MAHNOB-HCI [12] is a multi-modal dataset including synchronized recordings of video, audio, eye gaze data and physiological signals. The emotions are elicited by watching various video clips with different emotional keywords. The data was annotated with emotional tag (neutral, anxiety, amusement, sadness, joy, disgust, anger, surprise, and fear) and a 9-Likert scales on the arousal, valence, dominance and predictability dimensions using self-assessment.

The RECOLA corpus [4] contains spontaneous collaborative and affective interactions in French. The dataset was recorded in dyads during a video conference while completing a task requiring collaboration. The recordings include video, audio, ECG and EDA. The data was continuously annotated on valence and arousal dimensions. Additionally, a 7-Likert scale was used to describe the social behaviours on the five following dimensions: agreement, dominance, engagement, performance and rapport.

The EAGER Spontaneous 4D-Facial Expression Corpus [18] is the latest high-resolution spontaneous 3D dynamic facial expression dataset. The target emotional expressions include happiness, sadness, surprise, embarrassment, fear, physical pain, anger and disgust. The dataset consists of high resolution texture and depth, however it have not been made public available yet.

Although various corpus have been created, to our best knowledge, there does not exist any corpus that includes recording of spontaneous behaviours with both audiovisual and depth data that is also annotated continuously in multi-dimensional affective space. Another novelty of our multi-modal dataset is the chosen scenario: three way debate, this specific scenario was designed to replicate the commonly used Skype or Google hang-out type multi-video conversation. The scenario will not only allow the researcher to study the spontaneous affective state in relation to different modalities, but also enable the study of affect response between different participants. In addition, instead of capturing the dataset in a controlled laboratory environment, the capture is performed at various locations with different lighting conditions. A comparison of the recent publicly available datasets with our dataset is shown in Table 1.

Table 1. Overview of Human Affective Datasets. Types: P:posed, I:induced, S:spontaneous. Modalities: V:video, A:audio, D:depth, E:EEG, G:gaze, ED:EDA.

Dataset	Types	Subjects	Duration	Modalities	Annotation
SEMAINE (2008)[3]	I	20	04:11	V/A	Continuous
EAGER (2013) [18]	S	41	05:28	V/D	Discrete
Cam3D (2011) [13]	I	16	06:00	V/A/D	Discrete
MAHNOB-HCI (2011) [12]	I	27	06:00	V/A/E/G	Discrete
RECOLA (2013) [4]	S	46	06:30	V/A/E/ED	Continuous
DCU Affect Dataset	**S**	16	**05:30**	**V/A/D**	**Continuous**

3 Dataset Construction

3.1 Affective States Elicitation

In order to capture the spontaneous affective state, the debate scenario contained the following attributes: i) compared with other scenarios, the debate occurs naturally in everyday life, such as in a meeting, when watching a football match or movies. Participants are moved by real motivations leading to highly spontaneous affective state. ii) debate scenarios convey rich affective state and social behaviours such as conflicts, dominance, agreement/disagreement and interest/non-interest [23]. The following topics were selected for the debate:

1. How Ireland performed in the Six Nations Rugby match.
2. Should Ireland reduce the minimal wage?
3. Will Irish economy take off in the future?
4. Do humans have free will?
5. Do humans have a moral obligation to be vegetarian?

The first topic was used in two sections. The first section consists of three sports fans, allowing the capture of strong interest. The second section includes two sports fans and one non-sports fans, this will ensure the capture of rich interest and non-interest. The rest of the topics were used to enable the capture of agreement/disagreement, dominance, positive and negative valence.

3.2   Participants and Environment

16 participate from Dublin City University and Bell Labs Ireland were recruited for the dataset capture. The 16 participants consisted of 3 females and 13 males with an age group ranging from 20 to 50 years old.

Six offices with various background and illuminations were used during the dataset capture. In order to capture both facial expressions and upper-body gestures, each participant was arranged to sit 1 meter away from the screen.

3.3   Procedure

Each debate section consisted of 3 participants in which the 3 participants were first introduced to each other, then they were separated in three different offices and received an introduction on the experiment and an debate topic. Similar to [13], a wizard-of-oz method was used. Participants were told at the beginning of the experiment that their video and audio will be recorded for face and voice recognition. Without knowing the real objective of the experiment will avoid having participant exaggerate or mask their true affect state [13]. Each section will be ended either a time limit is reached (60 minutes) or the debate comes to a natural conclusion.

3.4   Multi-modal Data Capture Equipment Used

Due to the low quality of the Kinect RGB camera, a High-definition (HD) webcam (Logitech C910) was used and placed on top of the Kinect to collect the visual signals at each office. The microphones in the HD webcam were used to capture the audio signals and the Kinect was used to capture the depth information (As Shown in Figure 1).

Two computers were used in each office, one computer is used by the participant to communicate through each other using Google hang-out, while the other computer is used to capture the multi-modal data. The HD webcam provided 1280 x 720 px resolution colour images at 30 frames per second. The Kinect sensor consists of a normal RGB camera and an infrared camera. The RGB camera is able to provide 640 x 480 px color image and the infrared camera is used to capture the structured light and calculate 640x480 px 11-bit disparity map. A headphone was used by each participant to prevent the microphones capturing other participant's voices. In order to reduce the load on the hard drive, only the depth streams from the Kinect were recorded. The audio was recorded using the Microphone on the HD webcam at 16 bit 96kHz. Camera calibration was performed between the HD webcam and Kinect infrared camera in order to map the depth information to the RGB image. Because the video and depth signals are captured from different sensors subsequent manual synchronisation was required. The video stream was compressed using MJPEG. The depth stream was saved in ONI format which was developed and used by OpenNI framework, this allows the use of Natural Interaction for The End user (NITE) library to detect and track upper-body skeleton joints. The audio stream was saved as raw audio (PCM) format. Sample screenshot from the dataset is shown in Figure 2.

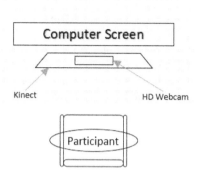

Fig. 1. Capture Environment Layout

Fig. 2. Sample screenshot from the dataset

4   Segmentation and Annotations

4.1   Segmentation

Due to each debate section usually last from 40 to 60 minutes long, the videos were segmented into 5 to 10 minute clips for easier annotation. We decide to choose the middle part from each section for annotation as the beginning usually consists of warm up chat while at the end of a section people might end up with discuss other topics. This results 34 video clips consists of approximate 5 hours and 30 minutes data.

4.2   Annotation Tool

Currently numerous tools have been developed with different features to annotated different type of datasets. European distributed corpora project Linguistic

ANnotator (ELAN) [19] is an annotation tool that allow user to create, edit, visualize and search annotations for video and audio data. Another widely used video annotation tool is **AN**notation of **VI**deo and **L**anguage (ANVIL) which was introduced in 2001 [20]. ANVIL is designed to annotate audiovisual material containing multi-modal dialogue. The FEELtrace is an annotation tool developed to enable the raters track the affect state via vocal and visual cues over continuous traces in the dimensional space [21]. FEELtrace allow raters watch the audio-visual recording and rate the perceived emotion sate by moving the mouse pointer within the 2-dimensional of valence-arousal space. The value of the affect state have been confined to [-1, 1] where -1 represent very negative (valence) or very passive (arousal) and 1 represent very positive (valence) or very active (arousal). More recently, the General trace (Gtrace) have been introduced to replace the FEELtrace with the ability to let people use their own dimensions and scales [22]. Due to the simple interface and continuous annotation support, Gtrace was chosen to annotate the data. Figure 3 shows a screenshot from the Gtrace annotation tool used.

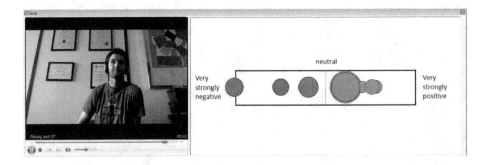

Fig. 3. Screenshot of Gtrace

4.3   Annotation Guidelines

Three independent annotators were hired, before the annotation task, each annotator was briefly introduced to the annotation task. Then they are required to complete a list of training tasks to test their affect recognition skill and to get familiarise with the use of Gtrace. The first task involves the identification of emotions expressions expressed on the face. The second task requires participants describing the emotional state showed in a video clip. The third task involves mapping a list of 24 emotional keywords to a valence-arousal 2-dimensional space. Task 4 involves annotating a list of sample videos from SE-MAINE dataset[3] use Gtrace.

Annotation was based on context-free observer judgment, each video clip was continuous annotated in 5 dimensions: arousal, valence, agreement, interest and content. To help the annotator better follow the conversation, the audio from each participant was mixed together.

5   Statistical Analysis

The annotations were first post-processed to remove duplicated annotations and then cropped to temporally align with the video sequences. For comparison purposes, the annotation data was binned with a frame rate fixed to match the video frame rate following the approach used in [4], which is a 33ms duration bin in our case. The percentage of positive frames, mean correlation coefficient and the Cronbach's alpha were computed for each dimension. The correlation coefficient measure the linear dependence between two variables, giving a value between -1 to +1, where 1 indicates total positive correlated, 0 indicates no correlation, and -1 indicates total negative correlated. The Cronbach's $\alpha$was used to estimate the internal consistency between annotations where $\alpha>0.7$ is considered as an acceptable internal consistency and $\alpha>0.8$ indicate good consistency. Due to the nature of the debate scenario, the raw data shows higher percentage of positive arousal (compare to the RECOLA corpus) and interest frames. The percentage of positive valence frames is similar to RECOLA corpus with lower internal consistency (See Table 2). The annotation also shows the capture of agreement and disagreement as well as positive and negative content. When annotated the data, the raters show much higher agreement on arousal and interest dimensions compare to valence, agreement and content dimensions (see Table 3).

Table 2. Compression of the statistics of the affective behaviours between RECOLA and our datset

Statics Properties	Arousal (RECOLA)	Arousal (Ours)	Valence (RECOLA)	Valence (Ours)
% Pos Frame	52.1	97.3	75.5	73.3
Mean Corr.	0.435	0.76	0.407	0.47
Mean α	0.80	0.89	0.74	0.66

Table 3. The statistics of the other three dimensions

Statics Properties	Agreement	Content	Interest
% Pos Frame	79.6	74.8	94.6
Mean Corr.	0.46	0.39	0.66
Mean α	0.63	0.60	0.83

6   Conclusions

A new 3D multi-modal spontaneous affect dataset has been introduced. 16 participants were recorded during a sequence of debates in a video conference, Skype style arrangement. Recording include video signals, audio signals and depth signals. Over five hours data have been manually annotated in 5 dimensions including arousal, valence, agreement, content and interest. The analysis of the annotations shows a good inter-agreement on arousal and interest dimensions and acceptable one for valence dimensions. The overarching goal behind the creation of this dataset is to provide a new rich annotated source of data that can be utilised by the research community for work in automatic human affect analysis. The dataset will be made public available for research purposes.

Acknowledgements. We would like to thank Patricia Scanlon and Philip Kelly for their supports during the dataset capture. This work is co-funded by Bell Labs Ireland and the Irish Research Council under the Enterprise Partnership scheme. The research that lead to this paper was also supported in part by the European Commission under the Contract FP7-ICT-287723 REVERIE.

References

1. Cowie, R., Douglas-Cowie, E., Tsapatsoulis, N., Votsis, G., Kollias, S., Fellenz, W., Taylor, J.G.: Emotion recognition in human-computer interaction. IEEE Signal Processing Magazine 18(1), 32–80 (2001)
2. Cowie, R., Schröder, M.: Piecing together the emotion jigsaw. In: Bengio, S., Bourlard, H. (eds.) MLMI 2004. LNCS, vol. 3361, pp. 305–317. Springer, Heidelberg (2005)
3. McKeown, G., Valstar, M., Cowie, R., Pantic, M., Schroder, M.: The semaine database: Annotated multimodal records of emotionally colored conversations between a person and a limited agent. IEEE Transactions on Affective Computing 3(1), 5–17 (2012)
4. Ringeval, F., Sonderegger, A., Sauer, J., Lalanne, D.: Introducing the recola multimodal corpus of remote collaborative and affective interactions. In: 2013 10th IEEE International Conference and Workshops on Automatic Face and Gesture Recognition (FG), pp. 1–8 (April 2013)
5. Cowie, R., Douglas-Cowie, E., Martin, J.-C., Devillers, L.: The essential role of human databases for learning in and validation of affectively competent agents. OUP, Oxford (2010)
6. Sandbach, G., Zafeiriou, S., Pantic, M., Yin, L.: Static and dynamic 3d facial expression recognition: A comprehensive survey. Image Vision Comput. 30(10), 683–697 (2012)
7. Kleinsmith, A., Bianchi-Berthouze, N.: Affective body expression perception and recognition: A survey. IEEE Transactions on Affective Computing 4(1), 15–33 (2013)
8. Aggarwal, J.K., Xia, L.: Human activity recognition from 3d data: A review. Pattern Recognition Letters (2014)
9. Pantic, M., Bartlett, M.S.: Machine analysis of facial expressions. In: Delac, K., Grgic, M. (eds.) Face Recognition, pp. 377–416. I-Tech Education and Publishing, Vienna (2007)
10. Gunes, H., Pantic, M.: Dimensional emotion prediction from spontaneous head gestures for interaction with sensitive artificial listeners. In: Allbeck, J., Badler, N., Bickmore, T., Pelachaud, C., Safonova, A. (eds.) IVA 2010. LNCS, vol. 6356, pp. 371–377. Springer, Heidelberg (2010)
11. Afzal, S., Robinson, P.: Natural affect data; collection and annotation in a learning context. In: 3rd International Conference on Affective Computing and Intelligent Interaction and Workshops, ACII 2009, pp. 1–7 (September 2009)

12. Soleymani, M., Lichtenauer, J., Pun, T., Pantic, M.: A multimodal database for affect recognition and implicit tagging. IEEE Transactions on Affective Computing 3(1), 42–55 (2012)
13. Mahmoud, M., Baltrušaitis, T., Robinson, P., Riek, L.D.: 3D corpus of Spontaneous Complex Mental States. In: D'Mello, S., Graesser, A., Schuller, B., Martin, J.-C. (eds.) ACII 2011, Part I. LNCS, vol. 6974, pp. 205–214. Springer, Heidelberg (2011)
14. Gunes, H., Schuller, B.: Categorical and dimensional affect analysis in continuous input: Current trends and future directions. Image Vision Comput. 31(2), 120–136 (2013)
15. Yin, L., Chen, X., Sun, Y., Worm, T., Reale, M.: A high-resolution 3d dynamic facial expression database. In: 8th IEEE International Conference on Automatic Face Gesture Recognition, FG 2008, pp. 1–6 (September 2008)
16. Schuller, B., Valstar, M., Eyben, F., McKeown, G., Cowie, R., Pantic, M.: AVEC 2011–the first international audio/visual emotion challenge. In: D'Mello, S., Graesser, A., Schuller, B., Martin, J.-C. (eds.) ACII 2011, Part II. LNCS, vol. 6975, pp. 415–424. Springer, Heidelberg (2011)
17. Schuller, B., Valstar, M., Cowie, R., Pantic, M.: AVEC 2012: The continuous audio/visual emotion challenge - an introduction. In: Proceedings of the 14th ACM International Conference on Multimodal Interaction, ICMI 2012, pp. 361–362. ACM, New York (2012)
18. Zhang, X., Yin, L., Cohn, J.F., Canavan, S., Reale, M., Horowitz, A., Liu, P.: A high resolution spontaneous 3d dynamic facial expression database. In: Proceedings of 10th IEEE International (2013)
19. Brugman, H., Russel, A.: Annotating multi-media/multi-modal resources with elan. In: LREC (2004)
20. Kipp, M.: Anvil - a generic annotation tool for multimodal dialogue (2001)
21. Schröder, M., Cowie, R., Douglas-Cowie, E., Savvidou, S., McMahon, E., Sawey, M.: 'FEELTRACE': An Instrument for Recording Perceived Emotion in Real Time. In: Proceedings of the ISCA Workshop on Speech and Emotion: A Conceptual Framework for Research, Belfast, pp. 19–24. Textflow (2000)
22. Cowie, R., Sawey, M.: GTrace-General Trace program from Queen's, Belfast (2011), https://sites.google.com/site/roddycowie/work-resources (Online; accessed April 29, 2014)
23. Vinciarelli, A., Dielmann, A., Favre, S., Salamin, H.: Canal9: A database of political debates for analysis of social interactions. In: 3rd International Conference on Affective Computing and Intelligent Interaction and Workshops, ACII 2009, pp. 1–4 (September 2009)

The Role of Color and Contrast in Facial Age Estimation

Hamdi Dibeklioğlu[1,2], Theo Gevers[1], Marcel Lucassen[1], and Albert Ali Salah[3]

[1] Intelligent Systems Lab Amsterdam, University of Amsterdam, The Netherlands
{h.dibeklioglu, th.gevers, m.p.Lucassen}@uva.nl
[2] Pattern Recognition & Bioinformatics Group, Delft University of Technology,
The Netherlands
[3] Department of Computer Engineering, Boğaziçi University, Istanbul, Turkey
salah@boun.edu.tr

Abstract. Computer based methods for facial age estimation can be improved by incorporating experimental findings from human psychophysics. Moreover, the latter can be used in creating systems that are not necessarily more accurate in age estimation, but strongly resemble human age estimations. In this paper we investigate the perceptual hypothesis that contrast is a useful cue for estimating age from facial appearance. Using an extensive evaluation paradigm, we establish that using a perceptual color space improves computer's age estimation, and more importantly, using contrast-enabled features results in estimations that are more correlated to human estimations.

Keywords: Age estimation, age perception, facial contrast, facial color.

1   Introduction

Age estimation is a perceptual task we perform automatically and often unconsciously, as a regulator of social interactions. Age estimation for youngsters is important to estimate cognitive capacities, whereas in general the age information would provide historical information usable in social contexts (e.g. "You certainly would not remember the time Commodore 64 was popular."). In many cultures, older individuals are accorded a certain respect associated with the age, and simultaneously, direct inquiry about a person's age is often considered inappropriate. The inevitable result is that the age is estimated from available cues, such as the appearance of the face, the tautness of skin and the existence of wrinkles, the color of the hair, the tone of voice, the manner of speaking, perhaps even the choice of clothing. It can be said that the human perceptual system is quite adept at making guesses about a person's age.

In this paper, we investigate the perceptual hypothesis that contrast is a useful cue for estimating age from facial appearance. Computer estimation of age from facial appearance has several applications, and it is important to establish reliable cues for this problem. While there is some evidence in perception studies that humans use contrast cues successfully for this task [14], it is known that many factors affect human perception of age: People are better at estimating age of younger faces or individuals that look like themselves, they are affected by the gender, attractiveness and expression of the estimated face, as well as biased by hair color, contextual cues, and such [20].

H.S. Park et al. (Eds.): HBU 2014, LNCS 8749, pp. 52–61, 2014.

Subsequently, an experimental approach is necessary to verify this hypothesis. In this paper, we describe a set of contrast features, and use a state of the art age estimation pipeline to test their usefulness for this problem. We report our results on the publicly available UvA-NEMO database with 400 subjects of ages 8-76 [2]. We establish that 1) using a perceptual color space improves computer's age estimation, 2) enabling contrast features marginally improves the results, although the improvement is more marked for approaches that process grayscale images, and more importantly, 3) using contrast-enabled features results in age estimations that are more correlated to human estimations.

Developing age estimation systems that model human estimation (rather than trying to estimate the true age) has not received much attention in the literature, but such systems are important for certain applications. One example is cosmetics, where the perceived age can be significantly reduced, hence comparisons are more meaningful with perceived age, rather than true age. Another example is the assessment of child exploitation crimes (e.g. child pornography), where an investigator gives a decision about the age of the child by inspecting visual images, and sometimes stakes his or her reputation on a decision, which is difficult to make [10]. In this case, a computer system that approximates the human age estimation can provide objective justification for such decisions.

2   Related Work

2.1   Psychophysical Studies

The few psychophysical studies on age estimation from face images suggest that contrast information from specific face regions and color distribution are indicative on the estimated age. Most studies employ digital manipulation of face images (predominantly females). In [4] this leads to the finding that removal of skin surface topography cues (such as fine lines and wrinkles), but preservation of skin color information, resulted in a decrease of estimated age of about 10 years compared with the age judgments of unmodified faces. In contrast, digital smoothing of facial discoloration resulted in a decrease of perceived age of 1 to 5 years.

In [1] the perceived age of male faces was studied using digital manipulation of shape and color information. While the authors could change the perceived age with color manipulation of individual pixels, they reasoned that this effect was not due to enhanced contrast or color saturation. In [8], skin wrinkling, hair graying and lip height were significantly and independently associated with how old a woman looks for her age. In a study on faces of Caucasian women [11], it was shown that the most important attributes to estimate age are eyes, lips and skin color uniformity. Another study on female faces [14] performed on the CIELAB color space indicates that faces with greater a* (red-green) contrast around the mouth, greater luminance contrast around the eyes, or greater luminance contrast around the eyebrows were judged to be significantly younger. These studies also point out to the importance of color information for age estimation.

2.2 Computer Estimation of Facial Age

In contrast to the findings reported in the previous section, the majority of computer based facial age estimation methods assume gray-scale images. This is partly the case because of the nature of the major benchmarking databases (such as FG-NET [19] and MORPH [16]), which collect old and new photographs of individuals, and consequently have varying degrees of color information in them. In this work, we partly mitigate this by exploring color information in our experiments on the UvA-NEMO database [2], which uses a controlled lighting setup. This database has a large number of subjects and a wide age range (8-76), but it does not allow longitudinal inspections of individuals.

The most important cues used in age classification are appearance-based, most notably the cranio-facial development, which instigated a host of methods that simulate the evolution of facial aging for analysis and synthesis [7,18], and wrinkles formed on the face due to deformations in the skin tissue [21,22].

The first class of methods apply subspace projection and manifold embedding techniques to find trajectories of age progression for a given individual. In [6] probabilistic kernel principal component analysis is used for this purpose. The second class of methods apply robust feature extraction approaches that are known to work well in face analysis, and treat the problem as a classification or regression task. In [21] Gabor wavelet features and local binary patterns were used successfully. Good surveys of the facial age estimation field can be found in [15] and [5].

3   Method

In this study, we propose the use of facial contrast with appearance information for automatic age estimation. The input images are assumed to have a moderately frontal face. The flow of the system can be summarized as follows. Initially, 19 facial landmarks are automatically located in the images. Then, by using the detected landmarks, size and rotation of faces are normalized, the regions of interest are cropped, and facial contrast features are extracted. To describe the facial appearance, uniform Local Binary Patterns (LBP) are computed on the input images. Finally, appearance and contrast features are fused to train/test Support Vector Machine (SVM) regressors.

3.1   Features

In the proposed system, facial appearance and contrast features are extracted from images and fused to improve age estimation accuracy as well as increasing the correlation between human perception and automatic estimation of ages. We use CIELAB color space in addition to gray-scale and RGB space, since it was designed as a perceptually uniform color space. It consists of an achromatic lightness channel (L*) and two color opponent channels a* (red-green) and b* (yellow-blue). In approximation, equal distances between two points in this space are also perceptually equal.

Before feature extraction, faces are normalized (with respect to scale and rotation) and regions of interest for facial contrast analysis are cropped using 19 facial landmarks (eyebrow corners/centers, eye corners, center of upper/lower eyelids, nose tip,

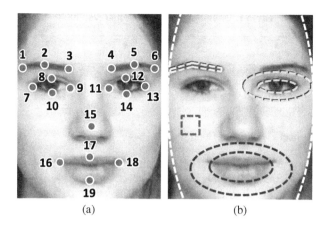

(a)   (b)

Fig. 1. (a) Used facial landmarks with their indices and (b) the regions of interest on an aligned/cropped face

lip corners, center of upper/lower lips, see Fig. 1(a)). These landmarks are automatically detected using the method proposed in [3]. This method models Gabor wavelet features of a neighborhood of the landmarks using incremental mixtures of factor analyzers and enables a shape prior to ensure the integrity of the landmark constellation. It follows a coarse-to-fine strategy; landmarks are initially detected on a coarse level and then fine-tuned for higher resolution.

Facial Contrast Features. To analyze and describe the facial contrast, we extract a set of features from eyebrows, eyes, lips, and whole face. First of all, eye centers are computed as middle points between inner and outer eye corners as $c_1 = \frac{l_7 + l_9}{2}$ and $c_2 = \frac{l_{11} + l_{13}}{2}$, where l_i shows 2D coordinates of landmarks. Then, the roll rotation of the face is estimated as $R_{\text{roll}} = \arctan\left(\frac{c_{y,2} - c_{y,1}}{c_{x,2} - c_{x,1}}\right)$, where $c_{x,i}$ and $c_{y,i}$ denote x and y values of center points c_i, respectively. Using the estimated rotation the pose is normalized to frontal face.

After normalization of rotation, face is cropped as shown in Fig. 2. Then, inter-ocular distance d_{io} (Euclidian distance between eye centers) is calculated and the face is scaled with a factor of $80/d_{\text{io}}$. Resultant normalized face image has a resolution of 200×160 pixels.

When the face is normalized, regions of interest are automatically determined, as shown in Fig. 1(b), using landmarks. Regional patches are adapted and modified from the age perception study of Porcheron et al. [14], where eyes, eyebrows, lips, and surrounding areas of those are manually annotated. In this study we automatically crop inner and surrounding regions of eye/lip by fitting an ellipse on the related landmarks. Inner eyebrow regions are cropped using the dilated lines on the eyebrow landmarks. Patches cropped on the cheeks are used as surrounding skin for eyebrows to cope with varying thickness of eyebrows and possible hair occlusions on the forehead. Surrounding regions define the skin, where the inner regions define feature areas. The boundary

Table 1. Definitions of the extracted features

Feature	Definition
Regional Mean Contrast:	$\frac{\text{mean}(I_{\text{skin}}) - \text{mean}(I_{\text{in}})}{\text{mean}(I_{\text{skin}}) + \text{mean}(I_{\text{in}})}$
Regional Median Contrast:	$\frac{\text{median}(I_{\text{skin}}) - \text{median}(I_{\text{in}})}{\text{median}(I_{\text{skin}}) + \text{median}(I_{\text{in}})}$
Inner (Michelson) Contrast:	$\frac{\max(I_{\text{in}}) - \min(I_{\text{in}})}{\max(I_{\text{in}}) + \min(I_{\text{in}})}$
Surrounding (Michelson) Contrast:	$\frac{\max(I_{\text{skin}}) - \min(I_{\text{skin}})}{\max(I_{\text{skin}}) + \min(I_{\text{skin}})}$
Inner Smoothness:	$\text{std}(I_{\text{in}})$
Surrounding Smoothness:	$\text{std}(I_{\text{skin}})$
Smoothness Rate:	$\frac{\text{std}(I_{\text{in}})}{\text{std}(I_{\text{skin}})}$

of face is also defined to compute global face contrast. Feature area for the face is the combination of the inner eyebrow, eye, and lip regions. Area lays between the face boundary and inner face regions forms the skin area of the whole face.

Let I_{in} and I_{skin} denote the one-channel (such as gray, R, G, B, L*, a*, b*) color values of inner and surrounding area of the related facial region, then facial contrast features can be defined as given in Table 1, where std denotes the standard deviation. The regional contrasts are defined as an adapted version of the Michelson contrast [9]. Note that the defined features are extracted separately for each of the face, eye, eyebrow, and lip regions. For eyes and eyebrows, average of the left and right side regions are used. Additionally, Michelson contrast and smoothness (std) features are extracted for the area within the face boundary. As a result, a 30 dimensional contrast feature vector is composed for the related color channel.

Appearance Features. To describe the facial appearance, uniform *Local Binary Patterns* (*LBP*) are used. The original *LBP* operator, which is proposed by Ojala *et al.* [12], takes the intensity value of the center pixel as threshold to convert the neighborhood pixels to a binary code. Computed binary codes describe the ordered pattern of the center pixel. This procedure is repeated for each pixel on the image and the histogram of the resultant 256 labels can then be used as a texture descriptor. In [13], Ojala *et al.* show that the vast majority of the *Local Binary Patterns* in a local neighborhood contain at most two bitwise transitions from 0 to 1 or 1 to 0, which is called a uniform pattern. Therefore, during the computation of the histograms, the size of the feature vector can be significantly reduced by assigning different bins for each of the 58 uniform patterns and one bin for the rest.

Each face is divided into 7×5 non-overlapping (equally-sized) blocks and uniform LBP descriptors are computed on each block (see Fig. 2). 8 neighborhood pixels (on a circle with a radius of 1 pixel) are used to extract the uniform LBP features. All these

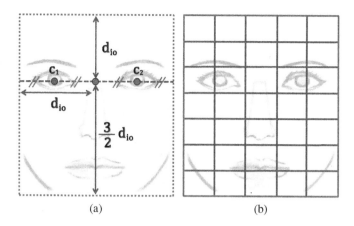

(a)   (b)

Fig. 2. (a) Scaling/cropping of a face image, and (b) the defined 7×5 blocks to extract appearance features

features are concatenated to form the appearance feature vector. Resultant appearance feature vector is $7 \times 5 \times 59 = 2065$ dimensional per color channel.

3.2 Classification

Extracted contrast and appearance features are concatenated for each color channel. Finally, features for the related color channels are fused. As a result, we have 2095 dimensional feature vectors for gray-scale, where the number of combined features for RGB and CIELAB is $2095 \times 3 = 6285$. Then these features are fed to SVM regressors for age estimation. In order to optimize the SVM configuration, different kernels (linear, polynomial, and radial basis function (RBF)) with different parameters (size of RBF kernel, degree of polynomial kernel) are tested on the validation set and the configuration with the minimum validation error is selected. The test partition of the dataset is not used for parameter optimization. The resulting estimation of the age is given as an integer with 1 year resolution.

4 Experimental Data

4.1 Face Images

To evaluate our system and assess the reliability of facial contrast and appearance information for age estimation, we extract and use the initial neutral frame of each video in freely available UvA-NEMO Smile Database [2] (see Fig. 3). The database has 1240 smile videos from 400 subjects (185 female, 215 male). Ages of subjects vary from 8 to 76 years. Videos were recorded (in RGB) with a resolution of 1920×1080 pixels at a rate of 50 frames per second under artificial D65 daylight illumination. Additionally, a color chart is present on the background of the videos for color normalization. Number of videos per subject varies from 1 to 4.

Fig. 3. Sample face images from the UvA-NEMO Smile Database

4.2 Age Perception

We gathered perceived ages for a subset of the neutral face images extracted from the UvA-NEMO Smile Database. The original recordings show a MacBeth Color Rendition chart. Using the black and white patches of the lightness scale in the MacBeth chart, we color corrected the images to have the same lightness values (L* in CIELAB color space), i.e. L*=96 for the white patch and L*=21 for the black patch, in the sRGB color profile [17]. In total, 84 face images were used from 42 male and 42 female, mainly Caucasian. Actual ages range from 8 to 76 years with a distribution similar to that of whole database. The face images were presented on a Eizo ColorEdge CG211 monitor which was calibrated to the sRGB standard.

Twenty-four participants, 14 male and 10 female, rated the perceived age of the (unknown) faces. All subjects had normal color vision as confirmed by the HRR color vision test and had normal or corrected-to-normal visual acuity. Participants' age vary from 18 to 55 years (average 31.6 years) and were of 6 different nationalities (Chinese, Dutch, Iranian, Italian, Polish, and Vietnamese). They were seated at a distance of about 0.5 meter from the monitor in a dimmed room. Using a slider bar they indicated the perceived age of the faces. Four different participants estimated the age of each face. The estimated ages by different participants, have been confirmed to be highly consistent (Cronbach's $\alpha > 0.87$). Average estimated age for each face is used as perceived age in this paper.

5   Experimental Results

In this section, we discuss the results of our experiments. First, we will discuss the accuracy of the system when only facial contrast and intensity (appearance) features are used, either individually or taken together. Then, the effect of color and contrast usage for estimating true and perceived ages will be analyzed.

5.1   Color, Contrast and Appearance

In this paper, we propose to combine facial contrast and appearance, and use perceptual color space CIELAB to increase the age estimation accuracy as well as improving the correlation between automatic estimations and perceived ages. However, it is also important to show the discriminative power of facial contrast and appearance, individually. For this purpose, we evaluate the individual and combined use of these features for different color spaces to estimate true age. In this experiment, a two level 10-fold cross-validation scheme is used on the whole set of the UvA-NEMO Smile Database. Each time a test fold is separated, a 9-fold cross-validation is used to train the system and select the regression parameters. There is no subject overlap between folds. The resulting *mean absolute error* (MAE) is given in Table 2.

Table 2. The MAE for true age estimation using contrast, appearance, and combined features

Features	Mean Absolute Error		
	Gray-scale	RGB	CIELAB
Contrast	9.50 (±8.31)	8.47 (±7.71)	8.41 (±8.04)
Appearance	6.12 (±4.87)	5.82 (±4.72)	5.81 (±4.59)
Combination	6.03 (±4.63)	5.59 (±4.52)	5.54 (±4.54)

Results show that enabling the use of color in the estimation of true age, noticeably improves the performance with respect to the use of gray-scale. CIELAB color space provides the most accurate estimations for both contrast, appearance, combined features. RGB performs slightly worse than CIELAB.

It is clear that using only facial contrast is not enough for an accurate age estimation system. In CIELAB color space, the MAE of using contrast features is 8.41 years where the MAE for facial appearance is only 5.81 years. Nevertheless, by combining the contrast and appearance features, the proposed system is able to achieve the best result with an MAE of 5.54. Combined features increase the accuracy approximately 4% and 5% (relative) with respect to appearance for RGB and CIELAB, respectively. However relative improvement for gray-scale is only 1.47%, which shows that gray-scale contrast is not as informative as color contrast.

5.2   Estimating True and Perceived Age

The aim of this study is to enable perceptual cues for age estimation to improve the correlation between automatically estimated and perceived ages. To this end, we analyze the effect of color and contrast usage for estimating true and perceived ages. As described in section 4.2, we collected perceived ages for 84 of 400 subjects. Face images of the remaining 316 subjects are used for training and validation. The regression parameters are selected using a 10-fold cross-validation on the training set. The trained systems are tested on these 84 subjects. Note that the true age information is used for training and validation in this experiment. Using appearance and combined features, the MAE and the correlation of estimations are computed for true and perceived ages. Reported correlation values are the linear correlation coefficients between the estimated ages and the true/perceived ages. Table 3 shows the MAE and the correlation for true and perceived age estimation using different color spaces.

Table 3. The MAE and the correlation for true and perceived age estimation

Features	True MAE Years (Correlation)		Perceived MAE Years (Correlation)	
	Appearance	*Combination*	*Appearance*	*Combination*
Gray-scale	5.98 (0.89)	5.79 (0.91)	6.52 (0.88)	6.11 (0.90)
RGB	5.46 (0.91)	5.23 (0.92)	6.24 (0.89)	5.08 (0.91)
CIELAB	5.38 (0.91)	5.09 (0.93)	6.08 (0.89)	4.09 (0.94)

Results show that enabling contrast features in the estimation of true age, decreases the MAE and increases the correlation by approximately 4% and 2% on average, respectively. For the estimation of perceived age, the combined use of appearance and contrast features, decreases the MAE and increases the correlation by approximately 19% and 3% on average, respectively. When we analyze the improvement rates, it is seen that the use of facial contrast shifts the estimations towards perceived ages. The relative MAE improvement, using the CIELAB color space, for perceived age estimation is approximately 5 times more than the improvement for true age estimation. Also, the use of color for automatic age estimation decreases the MAE noticeably, where the best accuracy is achieved by using combined features in CIELAB color space.

6   Conclusions

In this study, we have introduced the usage of automatically extracted facial contrast features and perceptual color space to improve age estimation and increase the correlation between automatically estimated and perceived ages. The majority of automatic facial age estimation methods focus on the appearance of the face, as the appearance is the most revealing aspect of aging. However, we show that facial contrast improves the estimation accuracy for both true and perceived ages.

Additionally, we evaluate the effect of using different color spaces on age estimation accuracy. Our results show that color-based features perform better than gray-scale. Besides, in our experiments, using perceptual CIELAB color space has provided the highest estimation performance for both true and perceived ages.

References

1. Burt, D.M., Perrett, D.I.: Perception of age in adult caucasian male faces: computer graphic manipulation of shape and colour information. Proceedings of the Royal Society of London. Series B: Biological Sciences 259(1355), 137–143 (1995)
2. Dibeklioğlu, H., Salah, A.A., Gevers, T.: Are you really smiling at me? Spontaneous versus posed enjoyment smiles. In: Fitzgibbon, A., Lazebnik, S., Perona, P., Sato, Y., Schmid, C. (eds.) ECCV 2012, Part III. LNCS, vol. 7574, pp. 525–538. Springer, Heidelberg (2012)
3. Dibeklioğlu, H., Salah, A.A., Gevers, T.: A statistical method for 2-d facial landmarking. IEEE Trans. on Image Processing 21(2), 844–858 (2012)
4. Fink, B., Matts, P.: The effects of skin colour distribution and topography cues on the perception of female facial age and health. Journal of the European Academy of Dermatology and Venereology 22(4), 493–498 (2008)
5. Fu, Y., Guo, G., Huang, T.S.: Age synthesis and estimation via faces: A survey. IEEE Trans. on PAMI 32(11), 1955–1976 (2010)
6. Geng, X., Smith-Miles, K., Zhou, Z.: Facial age estimation by nonlinear aging pattern subspace. ACM Multimedia, 721–724 (2008)
7. Geng, X., Zhou, Z.-H., Zhang, Y., Li, G., Dai, H.: Learning from facial aging patterns for automatic age estimation. ACM Multimedia, 307–316 (2006)
8. Gunn, D.A., Rexbye, H., Griffiths, C.E., Murray, P.G., Fereday, A., Catt, S.D., Tomlin, C.C., Strongitharm, B.H., Perrett, D.I., Catt, M., et al.: Why some women look young for their age. PLoS One 4(12), e8021 (2009)
9. Michelson, A.A.: Studies in optics. Dover Publications (1995)
10. Murphy, C.A.: The role of perception in age estimation. In: Gladyshev, P., Rogers, M.K. (eds.) ICDF2C 2011. LNICST, vol. 88, pp. 1–16. Springer, Heidelberg (2012)
11. Nkengne, A., Bertin, C., Stamatas, G., Giron, A., Rossi, A., Issachar, N., Fertil, B.: Influence of facial skin attributes on the perceived age of caucasian women. Journal of the European Academy of Dermatology and Venereology 22(8), 982–991 (2008)
12. Ojala, T., Pietikainen, M., Harwood, D.: A comparative study of texture measures with classification based on featured distributions. Pattern Recognition 29(1), 51–59 (1996)
13. Ojala, T., Pietikainen, M., Maenpaa, T.: Multiresolution gray-scale and rotation invariant texture classification with local binary patterns. IEEE Trans. on PAMI 24(7), 971–987 (2002)
14. Porcheron, A., Mauger, E., Morizot, F., Russell, R.: Faces with higher contrast look younger. Journal of Vision 11(11), 635 (2011)
15. Ramanathan, N., Chellappa, R., Biswas, S.: Computational methods for modeling facial aging: A survey. Journal of Visual Languages & Computing 20(3), 131–144 (2009)
16. Ricanek, K., Tesafaye, T.: Morph: A longitudinal image database of normal adult age-progression. In: International Conference on Automatic Face and Gesture Recognition, pp. 341–345 (2006)
17. Stokes, M., Anderson, M., Chandrasekar, S., Motta, R.: A standard default color space for the internet-srgb. In: Microsoft and Hewlett-Packard Joint Report (1996)
18. Suo, J., Zhu, S.C., Shan, S., Chen, X.: A compositional and dynamic model for face aging. IEEE Trans. on PAMI 32(3), 385–401 (2010)
19. The FG-NET Aging Database (2002), http://sting.cycollege.ac.cy/~alanitis/fgnetaging/index.htm
20. Voelkle, M.C., Ebner, N.C., Lindenberger, U., Riediger, M.: Let me guess how old you are: Effects of age, gender, and facial expression on perceptions of age. Psychology and Aging 27(2), 265 (2012)
21. Wang, J.-G., Yau, W.-Y., Wang, H.L.: Age categorization via ecoc with fused gabor and lbp features. In: Workshop on Applications of Computer Vision, pp. 1–6. IEEE (2009)
22. Zhan, C., Li, W., Ogunbona, P.: Age estimation based on extended non-negative matrix factorization. In: IEEE Int. Workshop on Multimedia Signal Processing (2011)

Dominant Motion Analysis in Regular and Irregular Crowd Scenes

Habib Ullah, Mohib Ullah, and Nicola Conci

University of Trento, via Sommarive 5, Povo (TN), Italy

Abstract. In this paper we present a novel method for dominant motion analysis in crowded scenes, based on corner features. In our method, we initialize corner features on the scene, and advect them through optical flow. Approximating the moving corner features to individuals, their interaction forces, represented as endothermic reactions in a thermodynamic system, are computed using the enthalpy measure, thus obtaining the potential corner features of interest. These features are exploited to extract the orientation patterns, used as input priors for training a random forest. The experimental evaluation is conducted on a set of benchmark video sequences, commonly used for crowd motion analysis, and the obtained results are compared against other state of the art techniques.

1 Introduction

More than half of the people of the world live in dense urban areas according to the report presented by Montgomery et al. [1]. Therefore, panic situations arising from events such as fire and riots in urban areas may threaten human lives thus making it necessary to carefully implement an evacuation plan. Real environments for such situations often include road networks, pedestrian pathways, and trails. The movement of pedestrians in the aforementioned places is a complex system to study. However, when we consider the environment being very large, all areas of the environment are not equally important.

For this purpose, a vision-based throttle that relies on the acquired visual data would be desirable in order to improve on the one hand the detection of behaviors in the crowd, and on the other hand the structure of the environment, for urban design and planning. However, the analysis of crowd motion is known to be a critical topic in machine vision, since most algorithms developed for object tracking are likely to fail in crowded scenes, due to multiple occlusions that make tracking of each single subject unpractical [2][3][4][5]. Therefore, the research has focused on considering the crowd as a single entity instead. These approaches often require low-level features such as multi-resolution histograms [6], spatio-temporal volumes [7][8][9], appearance, and motion descriptors [10].

Jacques et al. [11] and Zhang et al. [12] presented an overview about crowd motion analysis algorithms and associated issues. Qiu and Hu [13] exploit influence matrices of intragroup and intergroup to determine interactions among group individuals and between groups. However, no real-world data were used

H.S. Park et al. (Eds.): HBU 2014, LNCS 8749, pp. 62–72, 2014.
© Springer International Publishing Switzerland 2014

to validate the performance of the model. Zhang et al. [4] propose an approach for learning the semantic scene. For this purpose, motion patterns within each spatial block are learned by the Gaussian mixture model and motion patterns were clustered by a graph-cut algorithm. Rota et al. [14] exploit a particle-based approach to highlight particles of interest and group them based on their motion properties. Ozturk et al. [15] detect dominant motion flows by exploiting local and global information using SIFT features and Self-Tuning Spectral Clustering [16]. However, SIFT features can be unreliable in representing the characteristic parts of the objects due to redundant information in the 128-dimensional descriptor [17][18]. Moreover, the spectral clustering approach fails to simultaneously identify clusters at different scales [19]. In [20], the authors propose a block-based correlation approach for crowd motion segmentation based on orientation information. A more recent related work [21] extract motion patterns from a grid of particles which are used as a-priori information for CRF training to maximize the conditional likelihood. To better highlight the motion map, graph cut [22] is used by both approaches [20][21], subsequently. Although both methods perform well in crowd motion segmentation, they are not appropriate in detecting dominant motion flows, since the smoothness energy term in graph-cut is based on pixel intensities only. It is known that pixel intensities can be locally erroneous due to complex and untidy motion of the crowd [23]. Thus, in these cases, complex motion can affect the performance of graph-based approaches.

In this work we propose to address the problems mentioned above, by first extracting the corner features from a video frame and tracking them using the Lucas-Kanade optical flow. These features are then analyzed through an enthalpy model returning a subset of features of potential interest. Subsequently, we extract orientation information from the corner features and train a random forest to learn the behavior of the crowd, in order to detect dominant motion flows. In fact, compared to other approaches, such as CRFs and multilayer perceptrons, random forests deliver a higher level of predictive accuracy automatically, resist to overfitting, diagnose pinpoint multivariate outliers, and exhibit invariance to monotone transformations of variables.

2   Dominant Crowd Flows Detection

The method we propose consists of three main processing blocks namely: corner features extraction, corner features snipping with an enthalpy model, and random forest inferencing. During the first stage, corner features are extracted from a video frame. Motion patterns, defined in terms of velocity magnitudes, are extracted by tracking the particles using the pyramidal Lucas-Kanade optical flow [24]. In our approach we assume that each corner feature corresponds to an entity and has reactive forces upon other corner features surrounding it. Under this hypothesis, each feature can be classified not only on the basis of its own motion characteristics, but also in relation to the context, in this case provided by its neighbors. Therefore, we incorporate an enthalpy model from thermodynamics to identify potential features of interest only, since the emergent motion patterns in crowd dynamics have dynamical and physical interpretations in thermodynamics. During the last stage, the orientation features of the corner features act as input data to the random forest, so as to infer the dominant flows. The orientation features and the corresponding label sequence are used to learn the random forest parameters during the training stage, and the dominant flows are inferred on the test samples.

2.1   Corner Features Extraction

We selected corners as the main feature to analyze, since they represent peculiar elements in the scene and can be easily tracked in dense crowded scenes, leading to better consistency and accuracy in tracking, especially in scenes representing complex motion. The corner features are extracted from the video frame as shown in Fig. 1. To detect them, the function formulated in Eq. (1) is maximized.

$$E\left(u, v\right) \approx \sum_{xy} w(x, y)[I(x + u, y + v) - I(x, y)]^2 \tag{1}$$

Fig. 1. Corner features initialization. Frame from an irregular crowd video sequence (Left); the same frame with corner features driven (Right).

In Eq. (1), $w(x, y)$ is the window at position (x, y), $I(x, y)$ is the intensity at (x, y), and $I(x + u, y + v)$ is the intensity at the moved window $(x + u, y + v)$. The function in Eq. (1) can be reformulated as in Eq. (2).

$$E\left(u, v\right) \approx \left[u\,v\right] M \begin{bmatrix} u \\ v \end{bmatrix} \tag{2}$$

Where u is the displacement of the window w along x, and v is the displacement of the window w along y. The score R for a corner feature can be determined from the eigenvalues of the matrix M as formulated in Eq. (3).

$$R = \lambda_1 \lambda_2 - k(\lambda_1 + \lambda_2) \tag{3}$$

In the equation, k is a free parameter. A window with the greatest R is considered as a corner feature.

2.2 Enthalpy Model

The objective of this processing stage is to isolate and filter out the corner features that do not contribute to the identification of the dominant crowd flow detection. Motion information, defined in terms of velocity magnitudes, is extracted at regular intervals of K frames by tracking the corner features using the Lucas-Kanade optical flow [24].

The motion patterns observed in a crowded scene can be well modeled through a common thermodynamic measure, the enthalpy. Compared to the entropy model, which measures the disorder of a process, the enthalpy is a measure of the total energy of a thermodynamic system.

In thermodynamics, the enthalpy of a system with respect to temperature T and pressure P is formulated in Eq. (4).

$$dH = \left(\frac{\partial H}{\partial T}\right)_P dT + \left(\frac{\partial H}{\partial P}\right)_T dp \tag{4}$$

In a thermodynamic system, energy is measured with respect to some reference energy. Therefore, the internal energy U is calculated as a variation in U, instead of an absolute value as formulated in Eq. (5).

$$dU = \left(\frac{\partial U}{\partial T}\right)_V dT + \left(\frac{\partial U}{\partial V}\right)_T dV \tag{5}$$

It is worth mentioning that, compared to a thermodynamic system, the crowd dynamics represents a homogeneous system, which is clearly independent from the temperature. We consider the crowd as a continuum, simultaneously being able to capture motion properties of each corner feature at the individual level. It allows us to treat corner features as constituents (subpopulations) of the large crowd, each having its own motion properties. We thus have the possibility to examine the interactive behaviour between subpopulations, in the spatial neighborhood, which have distinct characteristics represented by the enthalpy model as formulated in Eq. (6).

$$H = U + pV \tag{6}$$

Here, U is the internal energy, p is the pressure, and V is the volume of the system. We exploit the kinetic energy in terms of internal energy, since we are only interested in motile corner features. *Pressure* is defined as $p = Force/Area$ and *Force* is $F = mass * acceleration$. For acceleration, we calculate the average velocity $\langle v \rangle$ in the spatial neighborhood over time, whereas the area A is the total number of corner features in the spatial neighborhood. Mass and volume of each corner feature may be associated with its contribution in the corresponding subpopulation, in the spatial neighborhood. However, we set them to 1 in our case to maintain consistency. Our enthalpy model is thus formulated in Eq. (7).

$$H = \frac{1}{2}mv^2 + \left(\frac{\partial \langle v \rangle}{\partial t}\right)\left(\frac{1}{A}\right) \tag{7}$$

Fig. 2. Interaction flow. The extracted corner features (left column); the same frame with the interaction flow overlayed (right column).

After evoking the relevant corner features using the enthalpy model, as depicted in Fig. 2, the orientation information of each corner feature in terms of angle of motion is extracted at regular intervals of K frames. We have selected 8 different directions quantized with a step of 45 degrees as depicted in Fig. 3, where R, TR, T, TL, L, BL, B, and BR stand for right, top right, top, top left, left, bottom left, bottom, and bottom right, respectively. The collected orientation features are stored to construct a feature vector for each corner feature. The feature vector is fed to the random forest classifier as an input (details are provided below) that in turn signals the corresponding label for the direction. To this end, a *tracklet* is drawn from the initial position to the final position of the corner feature where each pixel in the *tracklet* is assigned the same label. An example of a *tracklet* is shown in Fig. 4.

2.3 Random Forest

A random forest [25] is a classifier consisting of a set of tree-structured classifiers $\{h(\mathbf{x}, \Theta_k), k = 1,.....K\}$ where the $\{\Theta_k\}$ are independent identically distributed random vectors and each tree casts a unit vote for the most popular class at input $\mathbf{x}$. Given an ensemble of classifiers $h_1(\mathbf{x}), h_2(\mathbf{x}), \ldots, h_K(\mathbf{x})$, the margin function for the random forest over the input vector $\mathbf{x}$ and the label y is formulated in Eq. (8).

$$mg(\mathbf{x}, y) = av_K I(h_k \mathbf{x} = y) - \\ max_{j \neq y} av_k I(h_k(\mathbf{x}) = j) \tag{8}$$

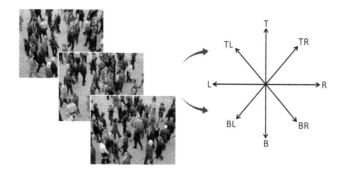

Fig. 3. Orientation-based dominant crowd flows detection. We analyze the crowd flows in eight possible directions according to the annotations on the left.

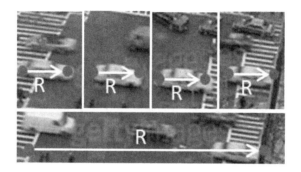

Fig. 4. Example. The top four frames show the motion of a corner feature to the right side of the image, while the bottom frame shows the computed tracklet.

In Eq. (8), $I(\cdot)$ is the indicator function. The margin measures the extent to which the average number of votes at an input $\mathbf{x}$ for the right class y exceeds the average vote for any other class. The larger the margin, the higher the confidence in the classification. The generalization error is given by Eq. (9).

$$PE = P_{\mathbf{x},y}(mg(\mathbf{x}y) < 0) \tag{9}$$

Where the subscripts $\mathbf{x}$, y indicate that the probability is over the $\mathbf{x}$ and y space. When the number of trees increases, the generalization error PE converges as in Eq. (10) for all the parameters $\Theta_1......\Theta_K$.

$$P_{\mathbf{x},y}(P_{\Theta}(h(\mathbf{x},\Theta) = y) - \\ max_{j \neq y} P_{\Theta}(h(\mathbf{x},\Theta) = j) < 0) \tag{10}$$

This means that random forests do not overfit as more trees are added, but produce a limiting value of the generalization error. A random forest specifies a particular label, given the observation sequence. Specifically, $\mathbf{x}$ is our input sequence, consisting in N observations collected within the K frames window (i.e. $\mathbf{x} = x_1, x_2, \ldots, x_N$), containing the orientation features. Given the observation sequence, the random forest signals the most probable label in terms of direction, inferring the output label y_m ($y_m = y_1, y_2, \ldots, y_M$) of the respective crowd motion direction.

During training, all the trees exploit the same parameters but on different training sets. These sets are generated from the original training set using the bootstrap procedure: for each training set, the same number of vectors are selected randomly as in the original set. Moreover, the vectors are chosen with replacement, meaning that some vectors will occur more than once and some will be absent. Only a random subset of variables are used to find the best split at each node of each trained tree. With each node a new subset is engendered. However, its size is fixed for all the nodes and all the trees.

3   Results

We have conducted the experiments on various crowd video sequences extracted from benchmark datasets, commonly used for crowd analysis, such as UCF [26][20] and UCD [21]. The video sequences in the UCF dataset are originally taken from Getty-Images, Photo-Search and Google Video. The video sequences in the UCD [21] dataset represent flows of students moving outdoor across two buildings. We have also downloaded two video sequences from YouTube (shown in the last two columns of Fig. 5.) to demonstrate the generalization properties of our proposed method. For each corner feature, the orientation features consist of a vector of $N = 4$ observations, where each element of the vector corresponds to the orientation information extracted after every $K = 8$ frames. The possible output directions are $M = 8$, one label every $45°$. We do not consider corner features with no motion. To evaluate the performance of our approach, we compared it with the application of the pure optical flow, as well as the methods recently proposed by [20] and [21] in Table 1. The first column presents the original video sequences, while columns (2 - 6) illustrate the ground truth, and the results obtained using the pure optical flow, the method presented in [20], the method presented in [21], and the proposed method, respectively.

To build the ground truth, individuals in the crowd have been manually annotated on each video. The ground truth consists of the number of individuals moving in each direction. By analyzing the ground truth, we notice that a significant number of people is moving only in limited directions instead of all eight directions. Therefore, we consider only four directions, where most of the people are moving, for the purpose of evaluation. For instance, the ground truth, TL-R-TR-L, for the first video sequence shows that most of the people i.e. 80 are moving in the top-left direction, while 54 people moving in the right direction stood second. There are 24 people moving in the top-right direction and 19 people moving in the left direction. To compare against the ground truth, orientation information is collected at each temporal window and accumulated over time for each video sequence for the reference approaches and the proposed

Table 1. Comparison of our approach with the reference approaches in dominant crowd flows detection. The first column presents the original video sequences and the second column shows the ground truth in terms of four dominant directions and the number of people moving in each dominant direction, respectively. Columns {3-6} present the reference approaches and the proposed approach.

No.	Ground truth	Optical flow	ICPRw[18]	ICIP[19]	Proposed
1	TL-R-TR-L	1	0	2	4
	80-54-24-19	25.76-18.33-8.07-21.41	7.75-79.68-0-11.91	43.81-18.88-11.64-16.53	52.38-15.3-13.19-12.26
2	R-L-TR-T/B	1	2	4	2
	40-35-15-12/12	17.74-17.82-15-17.86/6	46-13.4-1.89-4/11	41.64-29.78-8-5/3.63	45.87-33-2.98-3/5.23
3	R-BR-L-B	2	4	4	4
	70-34-28-15	34.66-20.40-21.82-6.97	62.50-27.99-5.66-2.53	48.5-27.76-20.4-1.57	43.87-29.66-24.63-1.09
4	R-BR-TL-TR	2	2	2	4
	100-60-57-29	32.48-7.17-8.86-9.81	47.59-26.23-2.87-8.51	52.26-21.58-7.43-11.38	73.78-13.1-5.9-2.65
5	R-L-TL-TR	0	2	2	2
	39-34-5-1	25.16-25.26-4.36-5.60	65.5-11.36-0-0	43.62-40.52-0.73-5.11	46.69-45.31-0.17-0.76
6	R-TR-L	1	1	3	3
	37-30-2	32.56-9.88-17.78	100-0-0-0	77.37-17.44-3.3	85.62-11.25-2.37
7	B-TL-BL-T	1	2	2	4
	58-42-9-5	17.97-24.33-3.44-26.47	13.73-3.72-9.34-1.79	43.43-44.4-4.85-1.39	45.83-37.13-8.66-1.37
8	R-T-L-B	1	2	4	4
	71-46-31-12	19.5-26.14-20.37-8.7	37.54-22.5-4.83-7.67	41.31-35.84-14.51-1.31	45.35-33.62-14.69-0.99

Table 2. Quantitative comparison of the reference approaches and the proposed approach with the ground truth in terms of accuracies. The first column shows a total number of 31 dominant directions, while other columns present number of correctly detected dominant directions along with percent accuracies by the reference approaches and the proposed approach.

Total	Optical flow		ICPRw[18]		ICIP[19]		Proposed	
	Correct	Accuracy	Correct	Accuracy	Correct	Accuracy	Correct	Accuracy
31	9	29.03%	15	48.38%	23	74.19%	27	87.09%

approach. To further clarify, frames from video sequences are depicted in the first row and the orientation information are annotated with different colors for the sake of visualization in the second row of Fig. 5, from the proposed method. In Table 1, the number of correctly identified directions along with orientation information in terms of percentages are provided for the reference approaches and the proposed approach. For the first video sequence, the pure optical flow collects 25.76% orientation information in the top-left direction, while 18.33% in the right direction, 8.07% in the top-right direction, and 21.41% in the left direction, respectively. Therefore, the pure optical flow correctly identifies one dominant direction, since the orientation information collected only in the top-left direction corresponds with the ground truth in terms of highest numbers in the same positions. Comparing our results with the reference approaches, we notice that our approach performs better or equally for most of the video sequences. In particular, our approach outperforms the reference approaches in video sequences, one, four, and seven, where it correctly identifies all four dominant flows. In Table 2, the number of correctly identified dominant directions along with the percent accuracies are presented by the reference approaches and the proposed approach, respectively. The first column presents the total number of dominant directions for all video sequences. The evidence for the surmountable performance of our approach lies in the fact that on the one hand the corner features combined with the enthalpy measure, highlights characteristic areas in the crowd, and on the other hand the random forest delivers a high level of predictive accuracy to detect dominant flows.

Fig. 5. Orientation information. Input frames from video sequences (first row); Orientation information annotated with different colors (second row), where each color is associated with a specific direction.

4   Conclusion

In this paper, we have proposed a novel method to detect dominant flows in crowd videos. The approach, comprising of three stages, extracts first corner features from a video frame, and then exploits the enthalpy model to analyze the corner features based on their motion properties. Orientation information is then extracted from the corner features and exploited to train a random forest. Dominant crowd flows are successively obtained in the testing stage. Experimental results on video sequences from two benchmark datasets, demonstrated that our proposal outperforms other state of the art techniques.

References

1. Montgomery, M.: The urban transformation of the developing world. Science 319(5864), 761–764 (2008)
2. Basharat, A., Gritai, A., Shah, M.: Learning object motion patterns for anomaly detection and improved object detection. In: International Conference on Computer Vision and Pattern Recognition. IEEE CVPR, pp. 1–8 (2008)
3. Ullah, H., Tenuti, L., Conci, N.: Gaussian mixtures for anomaly detection in crowded scenes. In: IS&T/SPIE Electronic Imaging, pp. 866303. International Society for Optics and Photonics (2013)
4. Zhang, T., Lu, H., Li, S.: Learning semantic scene models by object classification and trajectory clustering. In: International Conference on Computer Vision and Pattern Recognition. IEEE CVPR, pp. 1940–1947 (2009)
5. Ullah, H., Ullah, M., Conci, N.: Real-time anomaly detection in dense crowded scenes. In: IS&T/SPIE Electronic Imaging. International Society for Optics and Photonics (2014)
6. Zhong, H., Shi, J., Visontai, M.: Detecting unusual activity in video. In: International Conference on Computer Vision and Pattern Recognition, IEEE CVPR, p. II–819 (2004)
7. Kratz, L., Nishino, K.: Anomaly detection in extremely crowded scenes using spatio-temporal motion pattern models. In: International Conference on Computer Vision and Pattern Recognition, IEEE CVPR, pp. 1446–1453 (2009)
8. Laptev, I.: On space-time interest points. International Journal of Computer Vision, IJCV 64(2-3), 107–123 (2005)
9. Arslan, B., Zai, Y., Shah, M.: Content based video matching using spatiotemporal volumes. Internation Journal of Computer Vision and Image Understanding, CVIU 110(3), 360–377 (2008)
10. Andrade, E., Blunsden, S., Fisher, R.: Modelling crowd scenes for event detection. In: International Conference on Pattern Recognition, IEEE ICPR, pp. 175–178 (2006)
11. Jacques, J., Musse, S., Jung, C.: Crowd analysis using computer vision techniques. IEEE Signal Processing Magazine 27(5), 66–77 (2010)
12. Zhan, B., Monekosso, D., Remagnino, P., Velastin, S., Xu, L.: Crowd analysis: a survey. Machine Vision and Applications 19(5), 345–357 (2008)
13. Qiu, F., Hu, X.: Modeling group structures in pedestrian crowd simulation. Simulation Modelling Practice and Theory 18(2), 190–205 (2010)
14. Rota, P., Ullah, H., Conci, N., Sebe, N.: Particles cross-influence for entity grouping. In: Proceedings of the Signal Processing Conference, IEEE EUSIPCO (2013)
15. Ozturk, O., Yamasaki, T., Aizawa, K.: Detecting dominant motion flows in unstructured/structured crowd scenes. In: International Conference on Pattern Recognition, IEEE ICPR, pp. 3533–3536 (2010)
16. Zelnik-Manor, L., Perona, P.: Self-tuning spectral clustering. In: Advances in Neural Information Processing Systems, NIPS, pp. 1601–1608 (2004)
17. Chen, W., Zhao, Y., Xie, W., Sang, N.: An improved sift algorithm for image feature-matching. In: International Conference on Multimedia Technology, IEEE ICMT, pp. 197–200 (2011)
18. Wu, J., Cui, Z., Sheng, V.S., Zhao, P., Su, D., Gong, S.: A comparative study of sift and its variants. Measurement Science Review 13(3), 122–131 (2013)
19. Nadler, B., Galun, M.: Fundamental limitations of spectral clustering. In: Advances in Neural Information Processing Systems, pp. 1017–1024 (2006)

20. Ullah, H., Conci, N.: Crowd motion segmentation and anomaly detection via multi-label optimization. In: ICPR Workshop on Pattern Recognition and Crowd Analysis (2012)
21. Ullah, H., Conci, N.: Structured learning for crowd motion segmentation. In: International Conference on Image Processing, IEEE ICIP (2013)
22. Boykov, Y., Vekser, O., Zabi, R.: Fast approximate energy minimization via graph cuts. IEEE PAMI Transactions on Pattern Analysis and Machine Intelligence 23(11), 1222–1239 (2001)
23. Brunner, G., Chittajallu, D.R., Kurkure, U., Kakadiaris, I.A.: Patch-cuts: A graph-based image segmentation method using patch features and spatial relations. In: British Machine Vision Conference, BMVC (2010)
24. Yves, B.: Pyramidal implementation of the lucas-kanade feature tracker. Microsoft Res. Labs, Tech. Rep. (1999)
25. Breiman, L.: Random forests. Machine Learning 45(1), 5–32 (2001)
26. Ali, S., Shah, M.: A lagrangian particle dynamics approach for crowd flow segmentation and stability analysis. In: International Conference on Computer Vision and Pattern Recognition, IEEE CVPR, pp. 1–6 (2007)

Coupling Fall Detection and Tracking in Omnidirectional Cameras

Barış Evrim Demiröz, Albert Ali Salah, and Lale Akarun

Department of Computer Engineering, Boğaziçi University
Istanbul, Turkey
{baris.demiroz,salah,akarun}@boun.edu.tr

Abstract. Omnidirectional cameras have many advantages for action and activity detection in indoor scenarios, but computer vision approaches that are developed for conventional cameras require extension and modification to work with such cameras. In this paper we use multiple omnidirectional cameras to observe the inhabitants of a room, and use Hierarchical Hidden Markov Models for detecting falls. To track the people in the room, we extend a generative approach that uses probabilistic occupancy maps to omnidirectional cameras. To speed up computation, we also propose a novel method to approximate the integral image over non-rectangular shapes. The resulting system is tested successfully on a database with severe noise and frame loss conditions.

1 Introduction

Most of the current state-of-the-art action recognition methods work on videos or images acquired from conventional perspective cameras. Increased popularity of cheap RGB-D sensors such as Kinect also drew the attention of researchers to this modality for indoor scenarios and short-range action recognition. Omnidirectional cameras, compared to conventional cameras and RGB-D cameras, cover more ground and may eliminate need for multiple cameras. This property of omnidirectional cameras makes them appealing to use for action recognition purposes, especially for indoor scenes. These camera systems were indeed designed primarily for monitoring purposes, albeit by human monitors [1]. For automatic action and activity recognition, methods developed for conventional cameras need to be extended or appropriately modified to function under the assumptions and conditions introduced by the use of omnidirectional cameras.

In this work, we extend the probabilistic person localization approach proposed in [2] to omnidirectional videos. To illustrate the usefulness of the approach, we test it on a fall detection application. The person's location and fall state (i.e. standing or fallen) is tracked using a Hierarchical Hidden Markov model (HMM), where the images are the observations. We show that the proposed method is robust to occlusions, noise and missing data, while incorporating the information coming from different cameras.

This paper is structured as follows. Section 2 summarizes publicly accessible action and activity recognition databases using omnidirectional cameras.

H.S. Park et al. (Eds.): HBU 2014, LNCS 8749, pp. 73–85, 2014.

Section 3 briefly describes related work in camera-based fall detection. Section 4 describes the tracking framework we extend in this paper, and Section 5 proposes a fast integration scheme over foreground silhouettes to speed up computations. Our experimental results are reported in Section 6, followed by our conclusions.

2   Public Action and Activity Recognition Datasets Using Omnidirectional Cameras

There are not many public action recognition datasets involving usage of omnidirectional cameras. The *Opportunity* dataset has 72 sensors in total from 10 modalities, and two of these sensors are omnidirectional cameras [3]. There are 12 subjects performing various morning activities like preparing coffee, eating a sandwich, etc.

The high-level activities (e.g. preparing a sandwich) and low-level actions (e.g. reaching) are annotated in parallel tracks. There are four different tracks of annotations, first track determines the high level activities like preparing a sandwich, the second track contains walk, stand, lie and sit actions. The remaining tracks define actions of right and left hands: reach, move, release, stir, sip, bite, cut, spread, respectively.

In a more recent study, Behera et al. introduced a new dataset of egocentric actions [4]. A fisheye camera was mounted on the chest of a person and two sets of data were collected. One set contains 27 videos of tool usage, and the other is a 23 video set of "labeling and packaging bottles" scenario. Along with the omnidirectional videos, there are head mounted depth and RGB recordings of the same scene. At the time of this writing, ground truth was not available, but to be released soon. In the first set (27 videos) nine actions are recorded: take/put box, pick hammer, take/put baton, take nail, hammer nail, put down hammer, pick screwdriver, driving screw and put down screwdriver. The second set is a "labeling and packaging bottles" scenario, 9 actions in 23 videos are: pick and put bottle, stick label, pick and put box, remove cover, put bottle inside box, take and put cover, write address, take and put tape dispenser, seal the box.

The BOMNI-DB dataset by Demiröz et al. includes two sets of videos recorded in a room for action recognition purposes with two omnidirectional cameras at the same time [20]. We use this publicly available database in our study. The first set is a single person scenario, where the person performs the following actions throughout the video: sitting, walking, drinking, washing hands, fainting, opening/closing door. The second set involves multiple people performing the actions: sitting, walking, standing, handshaking, being interested in object.

3   Related Work in Fall Detection

Prevention and early intervention of falls in elderly are critical in ambient assisted living, and there have been numerous methods developed for this purpose [5]. Wearable sensors are widely used for fall detection; there are studies using sensors ranging from belts with pressure sensors to phones with 3-axis accelerometer [6,7]. On the other hand, cameras are less obtrusive and provide continuous observation. A broad survey of fall detection that includes vision modality among others is given in [8]. Here we focus only on visual approaches.

Most of the studies on camera-based fall detection in the literature depend on foreground segmentation, followed by an analysis of foreground height changes. In [9], motion history images from a single camera were used to quantify the motion of a person. But most approaches use more than a single camera, as the field of view imposes a limitation, and occlusions are always a consideration.

In an early approach, Nait-Charif and McKenna used omnidirectional cameras and modeled the person as an ellipse [10]. They have used particle filters to track persons, and considered unusual activities as cases of falling. In [11], wavelet transformation of the foreground's width-height ratio is used to model walking and falling using Hidden Markov Models (HMM). Audio features are used along with visual features to increase performance. Miaou et al. detected falls using width-height ratio of the single foreground area obtained [12].

Cucchiara et al. proposed a multi-camera approach for tracking a person and recognizing behaviors, including fall detection [13]. Using multiple cameras requires sophisticated tracking, particularly when the field of view of the cameras overlap. Omnidirectional cameras can sidestep this necessity.

In [14], the authors use two fixed, uncalibrated, perpendicular cameras. The main axis of the tracked object (i.e. the human) is computed, and used for inferring a fall. Similarly in [15], two cameras are used, independently, to detect the pose of a tracked person, and the motion information is integrated to detect falls. A recent approach by Kwolek and Kepski uses two Kinect cameras, one at the ceiling corner of the room, and the other at a one meter height [16]. This approach, like the conventional camera based approaches, is sensitive to camera placement to detect the fall events.

In the approach proposed in [17] the person is tracked and statistical outliers with respect to appearance and action are detected at different levels. Thus, an abnormal, horizontal position could be detected as a fall, if the spatial context is unexpected (e.g. on the floor, instead of the couch).

In a study using omnidirectional cameras, Huang et al. developed a rule based system that detects falls using the movement of the foreground segmentation over time [18]. They distinguish between radial falls (either inward or outward), and non-radial falls, as the appearance of the fall in an omnidirectional camera can vary depending on the action location. Over a dataset with 33 fall incidents, the authors report a 70 per cent detection rate. By injecting personal information like height, this rate can be increased to 80 per cent.

Contrasted with the related approaches, the method proposed in this paper has broad coverage in an indoor scenario, and is extremely robust to noise, occlusions and missing data. The next section describes the tracking methodology that forms the most important aspect of the approach.

4   Methodology

In this work, we track the inhabitants of an indoor scene using omnidirectional cameras and detect falls. We use multiple omnidirectional cameras to deal with occlusions. In [2], Fleuret et al. represented the ground plane with discrete, evenly spaced locations, and used a hidden location to handle transitions in and out of the scene. They have formulated a Bayesian framework to track multiple people, which utilizes the distance between the foreground segmentation image and a synthetic model of the human shape at any given location. Their model for a single person is an hidden Markov model (HMM), where the person's location is the hidden variable and images are observations. Our approach is built on Fleuret et al.'s foundations, and we extend their generative human shape model to fall detection in omnidirectional cameras.

Let L_t, F_t and I_t^c be a person's location, fall state of the person ($F_t = 1$ if fallen) and the image obtained from camera c at time t, respectively. Let bold letters indicate grouping of omitted indices, e.g. $\mathbf{I} = I_{1:T}^{1:C}$. At a given time, a person could be at one of the G locations, or at the hidden location that handles transitions in and out of the room. We are looking for the most likely value of the trajectory and the sequence of fall states of the person, given the observed images:

$$\{l_{1:T}^*, f_{1:T}^*\} = \arg\max_{l_{1:T}, f_{1:T}} \mathrm{P}(\mathbf{L} = l_{1:T}, \mathbf{F} = f_{1:T} \mid \mathbf{I}) \tag{1}$$

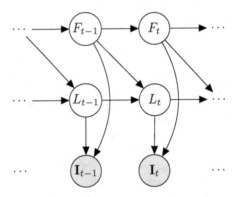

Fig. 1. The graphical model of the proposed system to detect falls. The variables F_t, L_t, I_t denote whether a person has fallen, location of the person and images obtained from all cameras at time t, respectively.

We can model the system using a Hierarchical HMM, given in Figure 1:

$$\mathrm{P}(F_t \mid F_{1:t-1}) = \mathrm{P}(F_t \mid F_{t-1}) \tag{2}$$

$$\mathrm{P}(L_t \mid L_{1:t-1}, F_{1:t-1}) = \mathrm{P}(L_t \mid L_{t-1}, F_{t-1}) \tag{3}$$

$$\mathrm{P}(\mathbf{I}_t \mid L_{1:t}, F_{1:t}) = \mathrm{P}(\mathbf{I}_t \mid L_t, F_t) \tag{4}$$

The problem stated in Equation 1 can be solved using the recursive Viterbi algorithm [19]. Let us define the maximum probability of observing the images and the trajectory ending up at location k and fall state s at time $t + 1$:

$$\Phi_t^{k,s} = \max_{\substack{l_{1:t-1} \\ f_{1:t-1}}} P(\mathbf{I}, \mathbf{L} = l_{1:t-1}, \mathbf{F} = f_{1:t-1}, L_t = k, F_t = s) \tag{5}$$

If we expand the expression we get:

$$\begin{aligned}
\Phi_t^{k,s} = &P(\mathbf{I_t} \mid L_t = k, F_t = s) \\
&\max_{r,d} \Big\{ P(F_t = s \mid F_{t-1} = d) \\
&P(L_t = k \mid L_{t-1} = r, F_{t-1} = d) \, \Phi_{t-1}^{r,d} \Big\}
\end{aligned} \tag{6}$$

The fall model is defined as:

$$P(F_t = k \mid F_{t-1} = i) = \begin{cases} 1 & \text{if } i = 1 \text{ and } k = 1 \\ z & \text{if } i = 0 \text{ and } k = 1 \\ 1 - z & \text{if } i = 0 \text{ and } k = 0 \\ 0 & \text{otherwise} \end{cases} \tag{7}$$

According to the model above, once fallen, the person will remain fallen. z is a small probability that denotes the probability of falling at a given time.

The motion model is defined as:

$$\begin{aligned}
&P(L_t = k \mid L_{t-1} = l, F_{t-1} = f) \\
&= \begin{cases} \dfrac{1}{Z} e^{-\rho \| l - k \|} & \text{if } f = 0 \text{ and } \| l - k \| < v \\ 1 & \text{if } f = 1 \text{ and } l = k \\ 0 & \text{otherwise} \end{cases}
\end{aligned} \tag{8}$$

The expression above states that if a person has fallen, his location does not change anymore. v defines the upper limit of walking speed, ρ fine tunes the average walking speed.

We assume that all the information is encapsulated in the binary foreground mask, and views are independent given the person's location. For a fixed time t, we write the generative model as:

$$P(\mathbf{I} \mid L = k, F = f) = P(\mathbf{B} \mid L = k, F = f) \tag{9}$$

$$= \frac{1}{Z} \prod_c e^{-\Psi(B^c, A_{k,f}^c)} \tag{10}$$

where B^c is the binary foreground segmentation obtained from camera c, $A_{k,f}^c$ is the binary image generated by putting the human silhouette in fall state f

at location k and $\Psi(\cdot)$ is a pseudodistance function which is defined for $A, B \in \{0,1\}^{\text{width} \times \text{height}}$ as:

$$\Psi(B, A) = \frac{1}{\sigma} \frac{|B \otimes (1 - A) + (1 - B) \otimes A|}{|A|} \tag{11}$$

An example of real foreground segmentation can be seen in Figure 2.

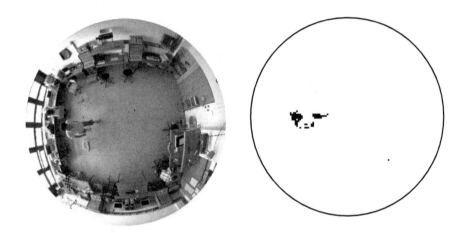

Fig. 2. Frame obtained from top camera and foreground segmentation of the frame

In this paper, human shapes are represented using a cuboid in 3D, instead of a rectangle in the 2D image as proposed in [2]. Example of human silhouettes represented as cuboids can be seen in Figure 3. However, doing this prevents the usage of integral images to speed up computation. Although our approach models a single person and the computations are tractable and fast, in the next section we describe a method to further speed up the pseudo-distance calculation.

5   Fast Integration over Silhouette Region

The method described in the previous section involves evaluation of $\Psi(B^c, A^c_{k,f})$ for all possible locations and states, hence constitutes the bottleneck of the algorithm. Notice that $\Psi(B^c, A^c_{k,f})$ can be expressed as:

$$\Psi(B^c, A^c_{k,f}) = \frac{1}{\sigma} \frac{|B^c| - 2|A^c_{k,f} \otimes B^c| + |A^c_{k,f}|}{|A^c_{k,f}|} \tag{12}$$

If the human silhouettes are straight rectangles, integral images can be used to speed up the computation of $|A^c_{k,f} \otimes B^c|$. However, in our case due to camera distortion and camera positioning human shapes cannot be represented as axis aligned rectangles. We represent human shape as a cuboid and further approximate the

Fig. 3. Locations in the room and the ideal foreground segmentation (human silhouette) for a human at location $k = 545$. Top: $f = 0$, the person is standing. Bottom: $f = 1$ the person has fallen.

silhouettes with multiple axis aligned rectangles; this way psuedodistance calculation can be carried out in constant time. An example of approximating silhouette with rectangles can be seen in Figure 4. Ideal human silhouettes and approximating rectangles need to be generated only once before tracking.

Let S be the region covered by a shape. The goal is to find a set of non-overlapping, axis-aligned rectangles, $\mathcal{R}^* = \{R_i\}_{i=1\cdots N}$, that minimizes non-overlapping area between S and rectangles. More formally:

$$\mathcal{R}^* = \arg \min_{\mathcal{R}} \Omega(S, \mathcal{R}) \tag{13}$$

where

$$\Omega(S, \mathcal{R}) = \left| (S \cup \bigcup_{R_i \in \mathcal{R}} R_i) \setminus (S \cap \bigcup_{R_i \in \mathcal{R}} R_i) \right| \tag{14}$$

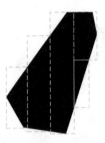

Fig. 4. Representing the human silhouette with five rectangles using the proposed method

Instead of finding the exact solution, we propose a method that iteratively splits rectangles and decreases non-overlapping area. $\mathcal{R}$ is initialized with axis-aligned bounding rectangle of the polygon. At each step, a rectangle with lowest fitness score is removed from $\mathcal{R}$ and split into two. To split a rectangle, the fitness score is calculated for top, bottom, left and right half of the rectangle. Second, the bounding rectangle of the half with lowest score and its complement is added to $\mathcal{R}$.

Fitness score of a rectangle R_i can be defined as inversely proportional to the area of non-overlapping region inside rectangle:

$$f(R_i) = \frac{1}{\Omega(S \cap R_i, \{R_i\})} \tag{15}$$

The fitness score above can be calculated in constant time using integral image of the shape.

We also define a tolerance value to enable early stopping when coverage is good enough. When $f(R_i)$ is greater than tolerance value, the approximation of R_i is considered as acceptable and R_i is not split any further. The number of rectangles covering the polygon can be chosen explicitly, because at each step the number of rectangles is increases by one. The algorithm and an example run can be seen in Figures 5 and 6.

6   Experiments

The proposed fall detection approach was tested on the BOMNI-DB dataset, which involves 5 sets of video pairs obtained using two omnidirectional cameras, containing fainting actions along with other actions of people [20]. Intrinsic and extrinsic camera calibration information is also provided along with the dataset where the camera model described in [21] is used. Each video is approximately 1.5 minutes long (about 750 frames). Videos typically suffer from high noise rates and severe frame loss. Moreover, the person is heavily occluded throughout the video. Keeping these properties of the dataset in mind, the videos can be

```
 1: procedure FINDCOVER(shape, maxRectCount, tolerance)
 2:      r ← bounding rectangle of shape
 3:      R ← {r}
 4:      if f(r) > tolerance then
 5:          return R
 6:      end if
 7:      while size(R) < maxRectCount do
 8:          r ← arg min f(r)
                   r∈R
 9:          R ← R \ r
10:          Calculate f() for top, bottom, left and right half of r
11:          r₁ ← bounding rectangle of the half with minimum score
12:          r₂ ← other half
13:          R ← R ∪ {r₁, r₂}
14:          if f(r₁) > tolerance and f(r₂) > tolerance then
15:              return R
16:          end if
17:      end while
18:      return R
19: end procedure
```

Fig. 5. Proposed algorithm to find rectangles covering a shape

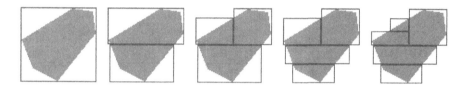

Fig. 6. An example run of decomposing a polygon into five rectangles. At each step, the rectangle with the greatest zero pixel count is selected and split.

considered challenging. When processing video pairs, to handle missing frames, a frame in one video is associated with the closest frame in time in the other video.

The proposed approach is compared with a baseline method (denoted as non-HMM here), which ignores temporal relations and maximizes the term in Eq. 10 for each frame separately.

The foreground detection is performed using the OpenCV 2.4.6 implementation of [22], where intensity value of each pixel is modeled using a mixture of Gaussians. The ground plane is discretized into 961 locations and in the motion model, the transitions from/to the hidden location are allowed only for the locations just in front of the room.

The tracking performance of the system is measured using Multiple Object Tracking Accuracy and Precision (MOTA and MOTP) metrics [23]. The distance between ground truth and prediction is expressed in terms of the overlap of their bounding rectangles. More formally:

$$d(R^{\mathrm{t}}, R^{\mathrm{p}}) = 1 - \frac{|R^{\mathrm{t}} \cap R^{\mathrm{p}}|}{|R^{\mathrm{p}}|} \tag{16}$$

where R^t and R^p are bounding boxes of the ground truth and prediction, respectively, and $|\cdot|$ is the area operator. The value of the threshold for accepting a prediction is selected as 0.2. Tracking results can be seen in Table 1. Since there is only one object to track, the *mismatch* component of MOTA is irrelevant, and therefore omitted from the table. In the table, *MOTP overlap* values are expressed as overlapping score, i.e. $1 - \text{MOTP}$.

Table 1. Tracking results on the BOMNI-DB. Improvements in terms of increased MOTA and decreased error over the baseline are indicated in green, whereas the occasional poorer result is shown in red.

#	Camera	MOTP	change	MOTA	change	miss rate	change	false+	change
1	top	0.57	+0.01	0.81	+0.05	0.09	-0.05	0.09	·
	side	0.58	·	0.88	+0.04	0.01	-0.06	0.11	+0.02
2	top	0.60	-0.01	0.94	+0.05	0.00	-0.03	0.05	-0.02
	side	0.53	·	0.94	+0.01	0.01	·	0.05	-0.01
3	top	0.59	·	0.95	+0.01	0.00	-0.01	0.05	·
	side	0.52	+0.01	0.96	+0.10	0.02	-0.09	0.02	-0.01
4	top	0.50	-0.01	0.89	+0.01	0.02	-0.05	0.09	+0.04
	side	0.48	·	0.97	+0.05	0.01	-0.03	0.02	-0.02
5	top	0.53	·	0.99	+0.01	0.00	·	0.00	-0.01
	side	0.47	·	0.98	+0.02	0.00	-0.01	0.02	·
OVERALL		0.54	·	0.93	+0.04	0.02	-0.04	0.05	·

The performance of the fall detection is measured by false positive and negative counts. False positive is a frame where a fall is reported when there is none. False negative is a fall frame reported as a non-fall. If a false positive or negative is closer than 4 frames (~half second) to the beginning of the fall event it is ignored, since annotations can be subjective at that scale. Fall detection results can be seen in Table 2. An example fall detection result can be watched at http://goo.gl/bZYOSw.

MOTP and MOTA values indicate that the proposed system performs tracking very effectively, with few errors. Using temporal information via hierarchical-HMM improves accuracy compared to the baseline method. The advantage of using HMM becomes more apparent in fall detection, in every video, falls are detected correctly. In case of HMM, false positives and negatives arise near the fall event annotation boundary, which may become subjective at sub-second resolution. However, the baseline approach produces false positives and negatives far from the true fall event.

We have also compared running times using multiple rectangles to represent silhouettes with using silhouette image itself. As it can be seen in Table 3, using multiple rectangles to represent silhouettes provides up to 7 fold speed up.

Table 2. Fall detection results on the BOMNI-DB. FP and FN stands for false positive and negative frame counts respectively.

#	Camera	non-HMM		HMM	
		FP	FN	FP	FN
1	top	156	20	0	0
	side	138	0	0	0
2	top	3	0	0	0
	side	3	0	0	0
3	top	4	0	0	0
	side	3	2	0	2
4	top	3	0	1	0
	side	1	0	0	0
5	top	1	0	0	0
	side	0	1	0	2

Table 3. Running times of the proposed method using the silhouette image (IMG) and using multiple rectangles (RECT)

#	IMG (sec)	RECT (sec)	speed up
1	340	51	×6.66
2	302	44	×6.86
3	259	38	×6.81
4	253	37	×6.83
6	308	44	×7.00

7   Conclusions and Future Work

In this paper, we have developed a tracking and fall detection system using omnidirectional cameras that is robust to noise, occlusions and missing data. The proposed system merges information provided from all the views and tracks the person. We report our results with a database that contains large amount of missing frames; by fusing multiple camera outputs, we obtain robust performance.

The integral image is a well-known technique for rapidly computing sum of pixel values in rectangular areas repeatedly. Because of the distortion introduced by omnidirectional cameras, they are not directly applicable in our case to rectangular human silhouettes. We have introduced a way to approximate human shapes as collections of non-overlapping rectangles to speed up pseudo distance computation. This scheme can be used to approximate the integral over arbitrary shapes on the image using the conventional integral image, which can be used in any domain where there is a need to compute pixel sums for arbitrary, non-rectangular shapes.

This paper described two methods that constitute useful tools for detecting and tracking people via omnidirectional cameras. As a future work, we plan to extend this framework to more actions, and to multiple subjects in the action scenario. The lack of datasets with detailed annotation is the primary hurdle in this area.

Acknowledgments. This research is supported by Bogazici University projects BAP-6531 and BAP-6754.

References

1. Yasushi, Y.: Omnidirectional sensing and its applications. IEICE Transactions on Information and Systems 82(3), 568–579 (1999)
2. Fleuret, F., Berclaz, J., Lengagne, R., Fua, P.: Multicamera people tracking with a probabilistic occupancy map. IEEE Transactions on Pattern Analysis and Machine Intelligence 30(2), 267–282 (2008)
3. Roggen, D., Calatroni, A., Rossi, M.: Collecting complex activity datasets in highly rich networked sensor environments. In: Networked Sensing Systems (2010)
4. Behera, A., Hogg, D.C., Cohn, A.G.: Egocentric Activity Monitoring and Recovery. In: Lee, K.M., Matsushita, Y., Rehg, J.M., Hu, Z. (eds.) ACCV 2012, Part III. LNCS, vol. 7726, pp. 519–532. Springer, Heidelberg (2013)
5. Salah, A., Gevers, T., Sebe, N., Vinciarelli, A.: Computer vision for ambient intelligence. Journal of Ambient Intelligence and Smart Environments 3(3), 187–191 (2011)
6. Bourke, A.K., O'Brien, J.V., Lyons, G.M.: Evaluation of a threshold-based tri-axial accelerometer fall detection algorithm. Gait & Posture 26(2), 194–199 (2007)
7. Noury, N., Fleury, A., Rumeau, P., Bourke, A.K., Laighin, G.O., Rialle, V., Lundy, J.E.: Fall detection-principles and methods. Engineering in Medicine and Biology Society 2007, 1663–1666 (2007)
8. Mubashir, M., Shao, L., Seed, L.: A survey on fall detection: Principles and approaches. Neurocomputing 100, 144–152 (2013)
9. Rougier, C., Meunier, J., St-Arnaud, A., Rousseau, J.: Fall Detection from Human Shape and Motion History Using Video Surveillance. In: Advanced Information Networking and Applications Workshops, pp. 875–880. IEEE (2007)
10. Nait-Charif, H., McKenna, S.: Activity Summarisation and Fall Detection in a Supportive Home Environment. In: ICPR, vol. 4, pp. 323–326. IEEE (2004)
11. Töreyin, B.U., Dedeoğlu, Y., Çetin, A.E.: HMM based falling person detection using both audio and video. In: Sebe, N., Lew, M., Huang, T.S. (eds.) HCI/ICCV 2005. LNCS, vol. 3766, pp. 211–220. Springer, Heidelberg (2005)
12. Miaou, S.G., Sung, P.H., Huang, C.Y.: A Customized Human Fall Detection System Using Omni-Camera Images and Personal Information. In: Distributed Diagnosis and Home Healthcare, pp. 39–42. IEEE (2006)
13. Cucchiara, R., Prati, A., Vezzani, R.: A multi-camera vision system for fall detection and alarm generation. Expert Systems 24(5), 334–345 (2007)
14. Hazelhoff, L., Han, J., de With, P.H.N.: Video-based fall detection in the home using principal component analysis. In: Blanc-Talon, J., Bourennane, S., Philips, W., Popescu, D., Scheunders, P. (eds.) ACIVS 2008. LNCS, vol. 5259, pp. 298–309. Springer, Heidelberg (2008)

15. Thome, N., Miguet, S., Ambellouis, S.: A real-time, multiview fall detection system: A LHMM-based approach. Circuits and Systems for Video Technology 18(11), 1522–1532 (2008)
16. Kwolek, B., Kepski, M.: Fall detection using kinect sensor and fall energy image. In: Pan, J.-S., Polycarpou, M.M., Woźniak, M., de Carvalho, A.C.P.L.F., Quintián, H., Corchado, E. (eds.) HAIS 2013. LNCS, vol. 8073, pp. 294–303. Springer, Heidelberg (2013)
17. Nater, F., Grabner, H., Van Gool, L.: Exploiting simple hierarchies for unsupervised human behavior analysis. In: 2010 IEEE Conference on Computer Vision and Pattern Recognition (CVPR), pp. 2014–2021. IEEE (2010)
18. Huang, Y.C., Rd, C.P., Li, C.: A human fall detection system using an omnidirectional camera in practical environments for health care applications. In: Machine Vision Applications, pp. 455–458 (2009)
19. Forney Jr., G.D.: The Viterbi algorithm. Proceedings of the IEEE 61(3), 268–278 (1973)
20. Demiröz, B., Eroğlu, O., Salah, A., Akarun, L.: Feature-Based Tracking on a Multi-Omnidirectional Camera Dataset. In: ISCCSP (2012)
21. Scaramuzza, D., Martinelli, A., Siegwart, R.: A toolbox for easily calibrating omnidirectional cameras. In: International Conference on Intelligent Robots and Systems, pp. 5695–5701. IEEE (October 2006)
22. KaewTraKulPong, P., Bowden, R.: An improved adaptive background mixture model for real-time tracking with shadow detection. In: Proc. 2nd European Workshop on Advanced Video Based Surveillance Systems, vol. 25, pp. 1–5 (2001)
23. Keni, B., Rainer, S.: Evaluating multiple object tracking performance: the clear mot metrics. EURASIP Journal on Image and Video Processing 2008 (2008)

Learning Sparse Prototypes for Crowd Perception via Ensemble Coding Mechanisms

Yanhao Zhang[1,2], Shengping Zhang[1], Qingming Huang[2], and Thomas Serre[1]

[1] Department of Cognitive Linguistic & Psychological Sciences
Institute for Brain Sciences
Brown University, Providence, 02912, USA
[2] School of Computer Science
Harbin Institute of Technology, Harbin, 150001, China
{yhzhang,qmhuang}@hit.edu.cn, {shengping_zhang,thomas_serre}@brown.edu

Abstract. Recent work in cognitive psychology suggests that crowd perception may be based on pre-attentive ensemble coding mechanisms consistent with feedforward hierarchical models of visual processing. Here, we extend a biological model of motion processing with a new dictionary learning method tailored for crowd perception. Our approach uses a sparse coding model to learn crowd prototypes. Ensemble coding mechanisms are implemented via structural and local coherence constraints. We evaluate the proposed method on multiple crowd perception problems from collective or abnormal crowd detection to tracking individuals in crowded scenes. Experimental results on crowd datasets demonstrate competitive results on par or better than state-of-the-art approaches.

Keywords: Sparse coding, Crowd perception, Biological vision.

1 Introduction

The perception of crowd behavior has become a popular area of study straddling multiple disciplines from cognitive psychology to computer vision. Over the years, several computer vision approaches to crowd perception have been proposed, drawing inspiration from disparate fields from sociology [1] to physics [2].

The so-called "social models" aim at characterizing the interaction between individuals in a crowd. This can be done explicitly using either systems of non-linear coupled equations as in the "social force" model [3,4] or implicitly via dynamic space-time correlations [5]. More recent work has extended some of these ideas using visual saliency [6], conditional random fields [7] or other energy-based approaches [8,9]. A measure of intended motion using space-time statistics [10] has been proposed as a model of people's "efficiency". The "collectiveness" of crowd scenes has been estimated using tools borrowed from machine learning including manifold-based similarity measures [11].

Representative physics-based approaches include methods based on chaotic invariants to represent people's trajectories [12] and methods based on stability analysis to identify different patterns of behaviors [13].

H.S. Park et al. (Eds.): HBU 2014, LNCS 8749, pp. 86–100, 2014.
© Springer International Publishing Switzerland 2014

Approaches borrowed from computational linguistic have also been applied to crowd perception including latent models [14,15] as well as bag-of-word and other related approaches for learning spatio-temporal occurrences of crowd motion patterns [16,17,18]. A notable approach based on the structural flow of scenes has been proposed in [19] and an approach for learning typical prototypes from correlations in atomic activities in [20].

Recently, several dictionary learning approaches have been proposed for learning crowd prototypes using sparse coding techniques [21,22,23] or closely related linear programming or matrix factorization techniques [20,24]. For instance, Lu et al. propose an efficient sparse coding approach for learning combinations of basis functions to detect abnormal events from pyramid video structures [22]. One of the main limitations with these methods is that they typically focus on modeling local motion patterns when patterns of crowd behavior tend to be more global. This leads to crowd representations that tend to be relatively unstable over time and fail to capture typical crowd peculiarities. This poses a challenge for applications ranging from the tracking of individuals in crowd to the recognition of crowd behaviors over long time periods.

Proposed approach and related work: Here, we investigate novel coding mechanisms to extend existing dictionary learning approaches with the aim to better capture the structural and collective characteristics of crowds. Our approach is motivated by recent developments in cognitive psychology, where it has been suggested that crowd perception may rely on pre-attentive ensemble coding mechanisms [25]. Human observers estimate the intended direction of briefly presented crowds of point-light walkers better than individual walkers. Such results have been taken as suggestive evidence that observers rapidly pool information from multiple walkers to estimate the movement of a crowd, very much in the spirit of feedforward hierarchical models (see [26,27] for reviews).

Feedforward hierarchical models of visual processing (including computational models of the visual cortex [28] and closely related convolutional networks [29]) have been shown to exhibit competitive performance for the recognition of individual human or animal activities. We propose a significant extension of a feedforward hierarchical model of the visual cortex [28] from the recognition of individual behaviors to group behaviors. Direction-selective motion units based on optical flow calculations are used as an input stage. Crowd prototypes are learned in intermediate stages of the motion processing hierarchy based on a sparse coding model. The proposed optimization learns crowd prototypes through ensemble coding mechanisms by jointly enforcing local structure and coherence in the input motion patterns.

Most closely related to our learning framework are learning approaches described above based on spatio-temporal representations of crowd motion patterns [5,15,30,31], structural flow [19] and correlations between atomic activities [20,11]. Compared to the original hierarchical model of motion processing [28], we show that the resulting learned prototypes are more selective and more easily interpretable. The overall hierarchical architecture leads to a compact visual

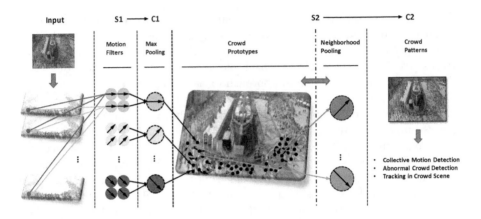

Fig. 1. Sketch of the proposed hierarchal model for crowd perception

representation capable of capturing the complex structure of motion patterns associated with crowd patterns.

In summary, this paper makes the following contributions: (1) We describe a novel mid-level representation together with an algorithm for learning crowd prototypes within a feedforward hierarchical model of motion processing; (2) motivated by biological considerations, we incorporate ensemble coding mechanisms within a dictionary learning approach via coherence and structural constraints to learn meaningful crowd prototypes; (3) we evaluate the proposed approach on multiple crowd perception problems from collective or abnormal crowd detection to tracking individuals in crowded scenes. Experimental results on crowd datasets demonstrate competitive results on par or better than state-of-the-art approaches.

2   The Approach

2.1   Hierarchical Model of Crowd Processing

An overview of the system is shown on Fig. 1. The basic visual representation is based on [28], which we only review briefly here. The model starts with motion-sensitive simple (S1) and complex (C1) units similar to those found in the primary visual cortex. In [28], Jhuang et al. compared several implementations of motion-sensitive S1 units. Here, we consider their implementation based on optical flow, because it is particularly amenable to extending existing approaches for crowd perception [2,5,15]. Specifically, we build a population of motion-sensitive simple (S1) units tuned to both speed and motion direction using the optical flow estimated from local space-time 3D volumes. Depending on the application (see later), these volumes are sampled either at random locations or at locations returned by the gKLT tracker as done in [11].

Let $\theta_{i,j}$ and $v_{i,j}$ denote the direction and velocity of the optical flow at image location (i,j). As done in [27,28], simple (S1) unit responses are then obtained using the following quantization:

$$r_{S1}^{i,j}(\theta_p, v_p) = \left\{ \frac{1}{2}[1 + \cos(\theta_{i,j} - \theta_p)] \right\}^q \times \exp(-|v_{i,j} - v_p|), \qquad (1)$$

where $\theta_p \in \{0°, 90°, 180°, 270°\}$ and $v_p \in \{3,6\}$ correspond to the preferred direction and speed of the unit, and the constant q controls the width of the tuning curve (here $q = 2$, see [27] for details). In the following stage, C1 unit responses are computed via a local max pooling on the S1 unit responses across both speeds and a local $l \times l$ spatial neighborhood.

In subsequent processing stages, units of higher visual complexity emerge after an additional *template-matching* (S2 units) as well as an *invariance-pooling* (C2 units) stage, increasing both the selectivity and invariance properties of the underlying model units. The response of S2 units is obtained by convolving C1 maps across all motion directions with a dictionary of stored prototypes. Originally, the dictionary of K S2 prototypes is learned via a simple random sampling procedure. Here, instead, we propose to learn crowd prototypes via sparse coding methods, which we describe next.

2.2   Learning Crowd Prototypes

Given a set of N input vectors $\mathbf{R} = [\mathbf{r}_1, \mathbf{r}_2, \ldots, \mathbf{r}_N] \in \mathbb{R}^{D \times N}$, learning a sparse dictionary of coding elements can be formulated as the following optimization problem:

$$\mathbf{B}^*, \mathbf{S}^* = \arg\min_{\mathbf{B}, \mathbf{S}} \|\mathbf{R} - \mathbf{BS}\|_2^2 + \lambda \sum_i \|\mathbf{s}_i\|_1, \text{s.t.} \quad \forall i, \mathbf{s}_i \succeq 0, \qquad (2)$$

where $\mathbf{B} = [\mathbf{b}_1, \mathbf{b}_2, \ldots, \mathbf{b}_K] \in \mathbb{R}^{D \times K}$ is a matrix that contains the learned basis functions as column vectors and $\mathbf{S} = [\mathbf{s}_1, \mathbf{s}_2, \ldots, \mathbf{s}_N] \in \mathbb{R}^{K \times N}$ is a matrix containing the corresponding linear coefficients. λ is a constant to control the tradeoff between the reconstruction error and the sparsity of the underlying representation.

We propose to incorporate the idea of ensemble coding in the form of two additional penalty terms embedded in Eq. 2. Cognitive psychology experiments have suggested the existence of pre-attentive pooling mechanisms used by our visual system to force chaotically moving crowds to cohere into a unified and visually appealing Gestalt. Psychophysics experiments have shown that participants rapidly pool information from multiple walkers to estimate the heading of a crowd [25]. Here we model this phenomenon via a *structural neighborhood cohesion* term, which forces input patterns to converge towards a similar interpretation and a *neighborhood manifold coherence* term, which incorporates explicit pooling mechanisms over output vectors to yield a locally more stable code.

These two constraints are embedded in the following optimization problem:

$$\mathbf{R}^*, \mathbf{B}^*, \mathbf{S}^* = \arg\min_{\mathbf{R},\mathbf{B},\mathbf{S}} \underbrace{\|\mathbf{R} - \mathbf{BS}\|_F^2}_{\text{recon. error}} + \lambda \underbrace{\sum_{i=1}^N \|\mathbf{s}_i\|_1}_{\text{sparsity term}} + \beta \underbrace{\sum_{i=1}^N \|\mathbf{r}_i - \mathbf{r}_i'\|_M^2}_{\text{structural term}}$$

$$+ \gamma \underbrace{\sum_{i=1}^N \sum_{j=1}^N \|\mathbf{s}_i - \mathbf{s}_j\|^2 \mathbf{W}_{ij}}_{\text{coherence term}}, \text{ s.t. } \|\mathbf{b}_k\|^2 \le c, k = 1,\ldots,K. \quad (3)$$

Here $\mathbf{r}_i'$ corresponds to the average over all $\mathbf{r}_i$ within the spatial neighborhood of unit i. λ, β and γ are constants used to trade the weights between the various regularization terms. The learning algorithm is initialized by setting up vectors of model C1 unit responses (tuned to different directions of motion over a local spatial neighborhood) as $\mathbf{r}_j$, such that $\mathbf{R}$ is the matrix containing all N C1 unit vectors as columns. $\mathbf{S}$ is the response of the S2 units.

In the above objective function, the first term is an estimate of the reconstruction error when encoding the S2 unit responses using the learned prototypes and associated coefficients. The second term corresponds to a standard sparsity constraint on the coefficients, which constrains the number of prototypes actually used to encode a given visual sample $\mathbf{r}_i$ to be small. We formulate the coherence constraint as a graph-based Laplacian regularization problem [32] while we formulate the structural constraint as a generalized Tikhonov regularization problem [19]. The coherence constraint should, in principle, help build a visual representation that takes into account the local manifold structure of the data enforcing local consistency of the flow. The structural term should help learn crowd patterns with locally similar trajectories from individuals. This can be also thought of as a denoising term effectively smoothing out the local motion flow towards a common vector $\mathbf{r}_i' \in \mathbf{R}'$ over a local spatial neighborhood (weighted by a Gaussian function over space):

$$\mathbf{r}_i' = \arg\min_{\mathbf{r}_i} \frac{1}{d} \sum_{j\in\mathcal{N}(i)} \exp(-\frac{\|\mathbf{r}_i - \mathbf{r}_j\|^2}{2\sigma^2}), \quad (4)$$

where $\mathcal{N}(i)$ denotes the set of indexes for the d nearest neighbors around $\mathbf{r}_i$ and σ is a constant.

Because the objective function in Eq. 3 is not convex with respect to $\mathbf{R}$, $\mathbf{B}$ and $\mathbf{S}$, we use a two-alternative minimization approach, alternatively optimizing one variable while fixing the others (see Algorithm 1). In step (A), the matrix of C1 response vectors $\mathbf{R}$ are computed after fixing $\mathbf{B}$ and $\mathbf{S}$. Eq. 3 can be rewritten by replacing the fixed term $\mathbf{BS}$ with $\mathbf{b}$ as detailed in the following matrix form:

$$\mathbf{R}^* = \arg\min_{\mathbf{R}} \|\mathbf{R} - \mathbf{b}\|_F^2 + \beta\|\mathbf{R} - \mathbf{R}'\|_M^2, \quad (5)$$

where $\|\mathbf{R} - \mathbf{R}'\|_M^2 = (\mathbf{R} - \mathbf{R}')^T \mathbf{Q}^{-1}(\mathbf{R} - \mathbf{R}')$ is the Mahalanobis distance between $\mathbf{R}$ and $\mathbf{R}'$. $\mathbf{Q}$ is the covariance matrix computed over $\mathbf{R}$.

Algorithm 1. Crowd prototype learning

---

1 **input:** Given N C1 unit reponse vectors $\mathbf{R} = [\mathbf{r}_1, \mathbf{r}_2, \ldots, \mathbf{r}_N] \in \mathbb{R}^{D \times N}$ and fixed parameters;

2 Initialize $\mathbf{B} = [\mathbf{b}_1, \mathbf{b}_2, \ldots, \mathbf{b}_K] \in \mathbb{R}^{D \times K}$ and $\mathbf{S} = [\mathbf{s}_1, \mathbf{s}_2, \ldots, \mathbf{s}_N] \in \mathbb{R}^{K \times N}$;

3 **repeat**

4 | **Step (A):**

5 | Given $\mathbf{B}$, $\mathbf{S}$, compute $\mathbf{R}'$ by pooling over the d nearest neighbors of $\mathbf{R}$ according to Eq. 4;

6 | Solve $\mathbf{R}^*$ via generalized Tikhonov regularization (Eq. 5);

7 | Update $\mathbf{R}$ with $\mathbf{R}^*$ (Eq. 6),;

8 | **Step (B):**

9 | Given $\mathbf{R}$, solve for $\mathbf{B}$, $\mathbf{S}$ (Eq. 8) using the *feature sign* search algorithm [33];

10 | Update $\mathbf{B}$, $\mathbf{S}$;

11 | Iteration number $i{+}{+}$;

12 **until** *Change in* $\mathbf{S}$ *between 2 successive iterations is smaller than* ε *or max iteration number reached*;

13 **output:** Optimized $\mathbf{R} \in \mathbb{R}^{D \times N}$, crowd prototypes $\mathbf{B} \in \mathbb{R}^{D \times K}$, S2 response coefficients $\mathbf{S} \in \mathbb{R}^{K \times N}$;

In Step (A), after the neighborhood pooling step (see Eq. 4) at each iteration, a closed-form solution can be computed using the generalized Tikhonov regularization as:

$$\mathbf{R}^* = \mathbf{R}' + (\mathbf{I} + \beta \mathbf{Q}^{-1})^{-1}(\mathbf{b} - \mathbf{R}'). \tag{6}$$

In Step (B), we follow the approach described in [32]. Let $\mathbf{W} \in \mathbb{R}^{N \times N}$ be a nearest neighbor indicator matrix ($\mathbf{W}_{ij} = 1$ if $\mathbf{r}_i$ and $\mathbf{r}_j$ are nearest neighbors and $\mathbf{W}_{ij} = 0$ otherwise). The degree of $\mathbf{r}_i$ is defined as $d_i = \sum_{j=1}^{N} \mathbf{W}_{ij}$ and $\mathbf{D} = diag(d_1, \ldots, d_N)$. This term can be rewritten as follow:

$$\sum_{i=1}^{N} \sum_{j=1}^{N} \|\mathbf{s}_i - \mathbf{s}_j\|^2 \mathbf{W}_{ij} = Tr(\mathbf{S}^T \mathbf{L} \mathbf{S}), \tag{7}$$

where $\mathbf{L} = \mathbf{D} - \mathbf{W}$ is the Laplacian matrix. By fixing $\mathbf{R}$ and incorporating the Laplacian regularizer, $\mathbf{B}$ and $\mathbf{S}$ can be updated according to:

$$\arg\min_{\mathbf{B},\mathbf{S}} \|\mathbf{R} - \mathbf{B}\mathbf{S}\|_F^2 + \lambda \sum_i \|\mathbf{s}_i\|_1 + \gamma Tr(\mathbf{S}^T \mathbf{L} \mathbf{S}),$$

$$\text{s.t.} \|\mathbf{b}_k\|^2 \leq c, k = 1, \ldots, K. \tag{8}$$

The above optimization is a typical laplacian regularization problem, which can be solved using the *feature sign* search algorithm [33]. As $\beta \to 0$, Eq. 3 degenerates into a typical graph-based sparse coding approach. Similarly as $\beta, \gamma \to 0$, Eq. 3 degenerates to a standard sparse coding optimization. In general, we have found the optimization procedure to converge quickly within 5 iterations (see Fig. 2 for a representative example). Thus, in all subsequent experiments we fixed the maximum number of iterations to $n = 5$.

(a) Sample convergence results on the Marathon sequence. Leftmost frame: standard optical flow followed by the prototype assignments for the first 5 iterations.

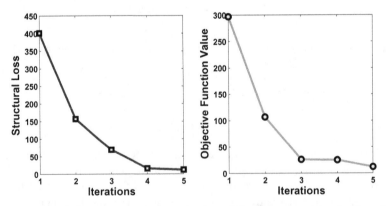

(b) Corresponding structural loss and value of the objective objective function.

Fig. 2. Illustrative convergence results for the proposed approach

Fig. 3. Representative examples of the learned prototypes. Shown are sample frames from the Collective Motion Dataset [11] overlaid with color coded symbols (best seen in color) indicating the closest prototype for the corresponding location.

Given a set of C1 unit responses **R** and a dictionary of prototypes **B**, one can compute the corresponding reconstruction coefficients **S** as S2 responses. Fig. 3 shows sample frames overlaid with symbols which indicate the prototype associated with the largest coefficient for that location. From visual inspection, it is clear that the learned prototypes are able to selectively capture a variety of crowd behaviors including crossing, lane forming, etc.

A sparse, invariant representation for crowd patterns can be obtained by computing the maximum coefficient over a spatial (and possibly temporal) neighborhood for each prototype at the next (C2) stage. In order to evaluate the effectiveness of the proposed approach, we carry out three experiments including: (1) the detection of collective motion patterns, (2) the detection of abnormal crowd behaviors and (3) the tracking of individuals in crowds. Additional results which could not be included because of space constraints can be found online at http:/serre-lab.clps.brown.edu/resource/zhangetalhbu2014.

3   Experiments

3.1   Abnormal Event Detection

Video dataset: We consider the UMN dataset (http:/mha.cs.umn.edu/Movies/Crowd-Activity-All.avi), which contains 11 video clips containing crowded escape video events acquired in 3 different scenarios. Each video begins with a normal behavior and ends with a panic escape. We resized all video frames to 120×160 pixels for computational efficiency.

Detection: For learning crowd prototypes, we sampled C1 unit vectors of size $5 \times 5 \times 4$ from the first 10 frames in each video sequence. Rather than considering random locations as in [28], we here sampled at keypoints returned by the gKLT tracker as done in [11] for crowds. We further pruned out vectors corresponding to locations with little activity by discarding vectors with a norm below a fixed threshold ($\theta = 0.1$).

We trained a dictionary of prototypes with $K = 30$. After the S2 stage, the maximum coefficient for each prototype over all locations and all frames were computed to yield C2 units, which can then be used as a compact visual representation for crowds. For classification, we used an SVM with an RBF kernel using the standard training/test data split to classify events as normal vs. abnormal and the accuracy measure described in [21].

Evaluating the different penalty terms: To assess the benefit of the different penalty terms in the proposed optimization function, we first sample a fixed set of C1 unit vectors to be used for all sparse coding based approaches. Fig. 4 shows a comparison of the system accuracy using different regularization terms: A basic Sparse Coding (SC) as described in [33] without either the coherence or structural constraint, two implementations of the proposed algorithm with the coherence term only (i.e., without the structural term) based on Laplacian Sparse Coding (LapSC) [34] and Graph-based Sparse Coding(GraphSC) [32] for varying

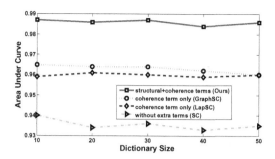

Fig. 4. Evaluation of the different penalty terms used in the proposed optimization function

Table 1. AUC measures for the detection of abnormal behavior on the UMN dataset

Method	Our approach	Cong et al. (SRC) [21]	Cui et al. (IEP) [8]	Mehran et al. 2009 (SF) [3]	Mehran et al. 2010 (SP) [9]	Optical Flow
AUC	**0.987**	0.99	0.985	0.96	0.90	0.86

dictionary sizes. It is pretty clear from this experiment that both constraints are indeed useful and that the proposed algorithm significantly outperform a vanilla sparse coding model.

Comparison with state-of-the-art approaches: Table 1 shows the accuracy of the proposed approach measured by the area under the ROC (AUC) together with a comparison with state-of-the-art approaches on the UMN dataset. Accuracy measures for the benchmark systems were those reported in the original studies [8,3,9,21]. The proposed approach achieve results that are on par or better than state-of-the-art systems including the Interaction Energy Potentials [8] (IEP), Social Force [3] (SF), Streakline Potential [9] (SP) and a standard Optical Flow (OF) based approach. The accuracy of our approach is only slightly lower than the Sparse Reconstruct Cost (SRC) method [21] despite the fact that the SRC uses MHOF as an input, which is much more robust to illumination, distortion and noise compared to the optical flow used here. Future work should compare the two approaches using the same exact inputs.

3.2 Collectiveness Classification

Video dataset: Here we consider the Collective Motion Dataset [11], which contains 413 videos from 62 crowded scenes including malls, traffic scenes, escalators, campuses, etc. Each video sequence contains 100 frames with ground truth annotations corresponding to 3 different levels of collectiveness — low, medium and high — obtained from 10 human observers. We used the same procedure as in [11] where a classifier is trained to discriminate between high vs. low, high vs. medium and medium vs. low.

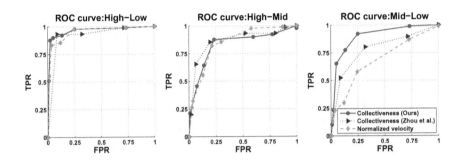

Fig. 5. ROC curves for the classification of collectiveness levels. We compare a "proto-type" score P derived using the proposed approach with a "collectiveness" score C and the "normalized velocity" V (see text for details).

Collectiveness score: For learning crowd prototypes, we sampled C1 unit vectors of size 8×8 ($\times 4$ directions of motion) as done in [28] from the entire database. Here, however, we sampled at keypoints returned by the gKLT tracker as done in [11] for crowds as opposed to randomly sampled locations as done in [28]. We further pruned out vectors corresponding to locations with little activity, i.e., vectors with a norm below a fixed threshold ($\theta = 0.1$) were discarded.

After the S2 stage, units are then pooled over a 8×8 spatial neighborhood to yield C2 units, which can then be used as a compact visual representation for crowds. We first consider an application to assessing the collectiveness of a crowd [11]. We used the C2 unit responses to compute a collectiveness metric score P as proposed by Zhou et al. [11]:

$$P = \frac{1}{|\Omega|} \sum \mathbf{e}^T((\mathbf{I} - z\mathbf{W}_p)^{-1} - \mathbf{I})\mathbf{e}, \tag{9}$$

where $\mathbf{W}_p$ corresponds to the adjacency matrix of the graph obtained by computing the χ^2 distance between C2 unit responses i and j over the set Ω. $\mathbf{e}$ is a vector with all elements set to 1.

Evaluation: Fig. 5 shows a comparison between the collectiveness score computed using the proposed representation (P) with two collectiveness score C and the normalized velocity V described in [11]. ROC curves are presented for 3 levels of collectiveness as done in [11]: Low, Medium and High collectiveness. For the High-Medium and High-Low categories, our prototypes perform on par with the state-of-the-art. This may reflect the ability of the proposed visual representation to distinguish different levels of dynamic motion, while preserving the consistency and structure of the crowd. Furthermore, our approach outperforms other approaches on the more challenging Medium-Low category.

3.3   Tracking in Crowded Scenes

Tracking framework: Because of the high similarity between targets and distractors, as well as the presence of significant occlusions, tracking in crowds is a

Fig. 6. Tracking results on 3 sequences for comparison between the proposed approach (circles) vs. the approach by Zhang et al [35] (squares). The ground truth is shown with dots. Tracking results for different subjects are marked with different colors.

very challenging problem. Classical single- and multi-target tracking approaches [35,5,15] have focused on extracting discriminative appearance models, often overlooking the problem of modeling the target's individual movement. These methods are usually based on a simple dynamic model with a smooth motion prior and additive Gaussian noise to predict the location of the target:

$$\mathbf{x}_{t+1} = \mathbf{x}_t + \mathbf{v}_t + \mathbf{n} \qquad (10)$$

where $\mathbf{x}_t$ corresponds to the target location, $\mathbf{v}_t$ the target 2D motion vector and $\mathbf{n}$ is Gaussian noise. Typically, $\mathbf{v}_t$ is computed using the state of the individual target from previous times, e.g., $\mathbf{v}_t = \mathbf{x}_{t-1} - \mathbf{x}_{t-2}$. Because of random jitter in the predicted target location, the computed motion vector is usually relatively noisy. Here, instead, we propose to compute the motion vector based on the average motion vector computed for all keypoints within the sampling region associated with the prototype with the highest assignment count. These prototypes are

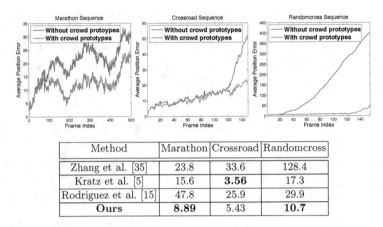

Fig. 7. Top: Average position error curves for the proposed sparse coding approach and comparison with baseline. Bottom: Comparison between tracking approaches using the average position error computed over entire sequences.

Method	Marathon	Crossroad	Randomcross
Zhang et al. [35]	23.8	33.6	128.4
Kratz et al. [5]	15.6	**3.56**	17.3
Rodriguez et al. [15]	47.8	25.9	29.9
Ours	**8.89**	5.43	**10.7**

learned by sampling C1 unit vectors for 5 consecutive frames with a dictionary of size $K = 8$. These samples are then updated over time and prototypes are learned anew for every frame. We implement a multi-target tracking algorithm for crowded scenes by extending the real-time tracker described in [35] as a base system. We extend this single-target tracker (originally based on a brute-force search approach) with a particle filtering framework.

Evaluation: We assess the accuracy of the proposed tracking approach and compare it to a baseline system, which also uses particle filtering, but with a simple state transition model (Eq. 10) as well as several state-of-the-art systems [5,15] for crowd tracking. Our evaluation is based on the crowded sequences used in [2,3]. Accuracy is measured by the Average Position Error (APE), which corresponds to the average difference (in pixels) between the position of the tracked object and the corresponding ground truth. Qualitative results are shown in Fig. 6 together with the average position errors for all methods in Fig. 7.

4   Conclusion

In this paper, we have extended a biological model of motion processing [28] from the recognition of individual human activity to group behaviors and described a new method to learn a dictionary of crowd prototypes. Motivated by human studies on crowd perception, our approach incorporates ensemble coding principles via structural and local coherence constraints within a sparse coding model. We have demonstrated the wide applicability of the approach to several problems in crowd perception. Experiments on public datasets demonstrate that the proposed model exhibits competitive performance against state-of-the-art approaches.

Acknowledgments. This work was supported by ONR grant (N000141110743) and NSF early career award (IIS-1252951) to TS. Additional support was provided by the Robert J. and Nancy D. Carney Fund for Scientific Innovation and the Center for Computation and Visualization (CCV) at Brown University. YZ and QH were supported in part by the National Basic Research Program of China (973 Program, 2012CB316400) and the National Natural Science Foundation of China (61025011, 61133003, 61300111, 61332016 and 61035001). YZ was funded by the China Scholarship Council.

References

1. Helbing, D., Molnar, P.: Social force model for pedestrian dynamics. Physical Review E 51(5), 4282 (1995)
2. Ali, S., Shah, M.: A lagrangian particle dynamics approach for crowd flow segmentation and stability analysis. In: CVPR (2007)
3. Mehran, R., Oyama, A., Shah, M.: Abnormal crowd behavior detection using social force model. In: CVPR (2009)
4. Pellegrini, S., Ess, A., Schindler, K., Van Gool, L.J.: You'll never walk alone: Modeling social behavior for multi-target tracking. In: ICCV (2009)
5. Kratz, L., Nishino, K.: Tracking with local spatio-temporal motion patterns in extremely crowded scenes. In: CVPR (2010)
6. Mahadevan, V., Li, W., Bhalodia, V., Vasconcelos, N.: Anomaly detection in crowded scenes. In: CVPR (2010)
7. Yamaguchi, K., Berg, A.C., Ortiz, L.E., Berg, T.L.: Who are you with and where are you going? In: CVPR (2011)
8. Cui, X., Liu, Q., Gao, M., Metaxas, D.: Abnormal detection using interaction energy potentials. In: CVPR (2011)
9. Mehran, R., Moore, B.E., Shah, M.: A streakline representation of flow in crowded scenes. In: Daniilidis, K., Maragos, P., Paragios, N. (eds.) ECCV 2010, Part III. LNCS, vol. 6313, pp. 439–452. Springer, Heidelberg (2010)
10. Kratz, L., Nishino, K.: Going with the flow: Pedestrian efficiency in crowded scenes. In: Fitzgibbon, A., Lazebnik, S., Perona, P., Sato, Y., Schmid, C. (eds.) ECCV 2012, Part IV. LNCS, vol. 7575, pp. 558–572. Springer, Heidelberg (2012)
11. Zhou, B., Tang, X., Wang, X.: Measuring crowd collectiveness. In: CVPR (2013)
12. Wu, S., Moore, B.E., Shah, M.: Chaotic invariants of lagrangian particle trajectories for anomaly detection in crowded scenes. In: CVPR (2010)
13. Solmaz, B., Moore, B., Shah, M.: Identifying behaviors in crowd scenes using stability analysis for dynamical systems. IEEE TPAMI 34(10), 2064–2070 (2012)
14. Hospedales, T., Gong, S., Xiang, T.: Video behaviour mining using a dynamic topic model. International Journal of Computer Vision 98(3), 303–323 (2012)
15. Rodriguez, M., Ali, S., Kanade, T.: Tracking in unstructured crowded scenes. In: ICCV (2009)
16. Lin, D., Grimson, E., Fisher, J.: Learning visual flows: A lie algebraic approach. In: CVPR (2009)
17. Kim, J., Grauman, K.: Observe locally, infer globally: a space-time mrf for detecting abnormal activities with incremental updates. In: CVPR (2009)
18. Andrade, E., Blunsden, S., Fisher, R.: Hidden markov models for optical flow analysis in crowds. In: ICPR (2006)

19. Zhao, X., Gong, D., Medioni, G.: Tracking using motion patterns for very crowded scenes. In: Fitzgibbon, A., Lazebnik, S., Perona, P., Sato, Y., Schmid, C. (eds.) ECCV 2012, Part II. LNCS, vol. 7573, pp. 315–328. Springer, Heidelberg (2012)
20. Zen, G., Ricci, E.: Earth mover's prototypes: A convex learning approach for discovering activity patterns in dynamic scenes. In: CVPR (2011)
21. Cong, Y., Yuan, J., Liu, J.: Sparse reconstruction cost for abnormal event detection. In: CVPR (2011)
22. Lu, C., Shi, J., Jia, J.: Abnormal event detection at 150 fps in matlab. In: ICCV (2013)
23. Zhao, B., Fei-Fei, L., Xing, E.P.: Online detection of unusual events in videos via dynamic sparse coding. In: CVPR (2011)
24. Zen, G., Ricci, E., Sebe, N.: Exploiting sparse representations for robust analysis of noisy complex video scenes. In: Fitzgibbon, A., Lazebnik, S., Perona, P., Sato, Y., Schmid, C. (eds.) ECCV 2012, Part VI. LNCS, vol. 7577, pp. 199–213. Springer, Heidelberg (2012)
25. Sweeny, T.D., Haroz, S., Whitney, D.: Perceiving group behavior: Sensitive ensemble coding mechanisms for biological motion of human crowds. Journal of Experimental Psychology: Human Perception and Performance 39(2), 329 (2013)
26. Crouzet, S.M., Serre, T.: What are the visual features underlying rapid object recognition? Frontiers in Psychology 2 (2011)
27. Giese, M.A., Poggio, T.: Neural mechanisms for the recognition of biological movements. Nature Reviews Neuroscience 4(3), 179–192 (2003)
28. Jhuang, H., Serre, T., Wolf, L., Poggio, T.: A biologically inspired system for action recognition. In: ICCV (2007)
29. Taylor, G.W., Fergus, R., LeCun, Y., Bregler, C.: Convolutional learning of spatio-temporal features. In: Daniilidis, K., Maragos, P., Paragios, N. (eds.) ECCV 2010, Part VI. LNCS, vol. 6316, pp. 140–153. Springer, Heidelberg (2010)
30. Zhang, Y., Qin, L., Yao, H., Huang, Q.: Abnormal crowd behavior detection based on social attribute-aware force model. In: ICIP (2012)
31. Zhang, Y., Qin, L., Yao, H., Xu, P., Huang, Q.: Beyond particle flow: Bag of trajectory graphs for dense crowd event recognition. In: ICIP (2013)
32. Zheng, M., Bu, J., Chen, C., Wang, C., Zhang, L., Qiu, G., Cai, D.: Graph regularized sparse coding for image representation. IEEE TIP (2011)
33. Lee, H., Battle, A., Raina, R., Ng, A.: Efficient sparse coding algorithms. In: NIPS (2006)
34. Gao, S., Tsang, I.W., Chia, L.T., Zhao, P.: Local features are not lonely–laplacian sparse coding for image classification. In: CVPR (2010)
35. Zhang, K., Zhang, L., Yang, M.-H.: Real-time compressive tracking. In: Fitzgibbon, A., Lazebnik, S., Perona, P., Sato, Y., Schmid, C. (eds.) ECCV 2012, Part III. LNCS, vol. 7574, pp. 864–877. Springer, Heidelberg (2012)

Dyadic Interaction Detection from Pose and Flow

Coert van Gemeren[1], Robby T. Tan[2],
Ronald Poppe[1], and Remco C. Veltkamp[1,*]

[1] Interaction Technology Group, Department of Information
and Computing Sciences, Utrecht University, The Netherlands
[2] School of Science and Technology, SIM University, Singapore
{C.J.VanGemeren,R.W.Poppe,R.C.Veltkamp}@uu.nl, RobbyTan@unisim.edu.sg

Abstract. We propose a method for detecting dyadic interactions: fine-grained, coordinated interactions between two people. Our model is capable of recognizing interactions such as a hand shake or a high five, and locating them in time and space. At the core of our method is a pictorial structures model that additionally takes into account the fine-grained movements around the joints of interest during the interaction. Compared to a bag-of-words approach, our method not only allows us to detect the specific type of actions more accurately, but it also provides the specific location of the interaction. The model is trained with both video data and body joint estimates obtained from Kinect. During testing, only video data is required. To demonstrate the efficacy of our approach, we introduce the *ShakeFive* dataset that consists of videos and Kinect data of hand shake and high five interactions. On this dataset, we obtain a mean average precision of 49.56%, outperforming a bag-of-words approach by 23.32%. We further demonstrate that the model can be learned from just a few interactions.

1 Introduction

In the past years, a lot of progress has been made in recognizing human actions from video [1]. Initial research has mainly taken a holistic approach, modeling the area of interest in the video as a feature. Bag-of-word approaches have become popular and suitable for the distinction of broad categories of actions such as running and jumping [2, 3]. By generalizing over specific poses, viewpoints and person appearances, they have been found to be fitting to data "in the wild". However, this generalization eventually hampers the use of these holistic approaches for the detection of more fine-grained actions.

Another approach to action recognition is to first estimate the configuration of the body, and then use this representation for subsequent action recognition. While classification can typically be performed more effectively, the challenge of dealing with less-controlled videos is moved to the body pose estimation process.

---

* This publication was supported by the Dutch national program COMMIT.

H.S. Park et al. (Eds.): HBU 2014, LNCS 8749, pp. 101–115, 2014.
© Springer International Publishing Switzerland 2014

Recently, a lot of progress has been made. Notably, the introduction of pictorial structure models [4–6] and poselets [7] have paved the way for robust estimation of body poses in "in the wild". One challenge that remains is how to deal with the variations in the performance of an action. The same action can be performed in many ways and still be perceived as the same action. For example, sitting down will be performed differently depending on whether the person will sit on a barstool or on a chair. Another issue is that not all body parts contribute equally in the performance of an arbitrary action. For some actions (e.g. pointing), the position of the legs is not that important. This is also typically the case when a person interacts with another person or with the environment.

In this paper, we focus on the detection and recognition of dyadic interactions from video. These interactions are coordinated in a sense that the movement of one person depends on the movement of the other, and *vice versa*. For example, a hand shake requires both people to face each other, extend their arms forward, grab the other's hand and simultaneously move the hands up and down. If the shake of the hands would not be coordinated, we would probably not perceive the movements as a hand shake. Recognizing coordinated interactions therefore does not only require the detection of the movement of both persons individually, but also the assessment of the coordination of their movements. This notion is reflected in the approach proposed in this paper.

We start by detecting individual actions using poselets, which are templates that encode the specific configuration of parts of the body. Poselets are typically described using histograms of oriented gradients (HOG). Maji *et al.* [8] have used poselets for the recognition of actions from a single frame. In contrast, we consider videos and take advantage of the movement information by including histograms of oriented flow (HOF) information into the poselet representation, as in [9]. Yao *et al.* [10] also use a combination of HOG and HOF to recognize actions. They use a grammar-like representation in which the HOF determines transitions between different poses, encoded using HOG. In this formulation, temporal variations in the performance of an action can be overcome.

In this work, we estimate the locations of key joints from the poselet detections. The relative positions are learned during training using 2D joint positions estimated by Kinect. When the estimated joint positions of two persons are close, we further investigate the area. For example, to detect a hand shake, the right hand joints are the key joints and the overlapping area contains both hands. We encode this area with a combination of HOG and HOF and train a classifier for the interaction. This allows us to analyze the interaction at a more fine-grained level. During testing, only video data is used, making the approach suitable for the detection of dyadic actions in a wide range of applications, from surveillance to the fine-grained analysis of people in conversation. We evaluate our approach on *ShakeFive*, a novel dataset containing hand shakes and high fives, as well as the metadata gathered from Kinect.

Our model assumes that the scene is recorded by a static camera and actions are viewed from the side. We also assume that no occlusions occur in recording the interaction. We restrict ourselves in this manner because we are first and foremost interested in the the ability to learn pictorial structures using Kinect, while recognizing the interactions without the use of hardware other than a standard camera.

We make the following contributions: First, we train a dyadic interaction recognition model using Kinect information in a controlled environment during training, while using the model to recognize dyadic interactions from the video data only. Second, we demonstrate that fine-grained analysis of the interaction around key joints is beneficial to the classification of these interactions. Finally, we provide a new dataset containing video and joint poses from Kinect of two individuals involved in a hand shake or a high five.

The paper is structured as follows. First, we discuss related work. In Section 3, we present our approach. We outline and discuss our experiments in Section 4 and conclude in Section 5.

2   Related Work

One popular approach to recognize actions from video is based on a bag-of-words representation. Distinct features based on edges, motion or both are found and collected within spatio-temporal regions of a video. While the recent trend to rely on trajectories of these points has shown potential, there is typically no connection between the features and the articulated human body. As a consequence, it is difficult to distinguish between actions that differ slightly. We can imagine, for instance, that running a hand through the hair is indistinguishable from scratching the head even though both are performed in different contexts. We therefore focus here on approaches that consider body poses as an intermediary level, to allow a more fine-grained analysis. We discuss recent work in this area, with a specific focus on their application for the classification of interactions between people.

While body poses are a convenient representation to learn actions from, there is typically a challenge in recovering these body poses from video. Body part models that encode both the appearance of individual body parts and the spatial relations between them have shown increasing invariance to nuisance factors. One particularly popular representation is based on the pictorial structures model [5, 6], where a template is associated to each body part. The articulation of one body part in relation to another in encoded as a relation orientation between the two. Often, a particular configuration of two or more body parts together is especially informative of the pose, and typically more easily detectable than the body parts independently. This idea gave rise to the introduction of poselets [7], templates that encode a specific configuration of body parts such as a bent arm. While poselets where initially used to detect humans, they have been employed for action detection from still images as well [8]. Such an approach works well for poses that are typical for a certain action, but it is less suitable for actions associated with arbitrary poses, without additional motion information.

Actions are not only characterizable by their pose or shape, but also by their movement over time. Jhuang *et al.* [11] show that movement at specific joint locations gives strong cues for action recognition. Raptis and Sigal [9] include an optical flow term in their reformulation of poselets to recognize actions from video. In a related work by Yao et al. [10], optical flow is used to model transitions from one class of postures to the next. Effectively, this approach allows to detect actions that vary in their execution in time, such as interactions with a vending machine. There can be variation in the spatial performance of actions due to the environment. Reaching actions depend on the location of the object, and some have addressed this using object detections as cues for action recognition (e.g. [12, 13]). Actions can also have a social component if they are performed together with others. These actions are typically coordinated in the sense that movements of one person are affected by, and affect, the movements of others. In daily life, there are many coordinated interactions, such as walking hand-in-hand, dancing, shaking hands and fighting. Typically, the relative positions of people in the scene give rise to the understanding of interactions or group actions. Lan et al. [14] introduce the action context descriptor that encodes both the estimated action performed by the person under focus, and those in his vicinity. Choi et al. [15] address learning automatically the parameters of this vicinity in terms of size, distance and the division into discrete orientations. Besides people's relative positions, cues from people's orientation [16] and movements [17] can further help in understanding group activities. While much progress has been made in understanding these activities, the main focus is on broad action categories such as queueing or fighting. A notable exception is the work of Patron-Perez et al. [18], who focused on dyadic interactions such as hand shakes and hugs. However, they use upper body detectors and head pose classifiers without fine-grained limb movement information.

In these dyadic interactions, the movements of two people can be so tightly coordinated that it is intrinsically part of the interaction. For example, a hand shake would not be recognized if the two hands involved would not move in unison. Similarly, walking side-by-side and walking hand-in-hand are largely similar but differ in the coordination of the movements of the hands. Making a fine-grained distinction helps in understanding interactions, and the relations between people. From a detection perspective, it requires not only the detection of the actions of each individual involved in the interaction, but also the coordination of their movements. Often, there is a limited number of key joints or body parts involved. For a hand shake, these are typically the right hands of both interactants. In this paper, we introduce a method that builds on previous work in individual action recognition and extends it to detect fine-grained, coordinated interactions between two people.

3   Dyadic Interaction Detection

We present in this section our method to learn the poselet model to detect, in time and space, dyadic interactions from video. In the training phase, we also use Kinect information, to speed-up the learning of the poselets. A detection model is learned for each action individually. We discuss the training and evaluation of the models in the subsequent sections.

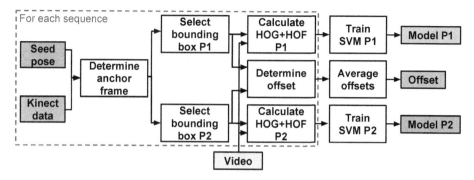

Fig. 1. Pipeline for learning the detection models for the two people involved in the interaction, and the spatial offset between the models. See text for details.

3.1   Training Action Models from Video and Kinect Data

In Figure 1 we show an overview of our pipeline for training the interaction models. We can identify four main parts in the pipeline which we will discuss one by one: first we determine the anchor frame to acquire the most invariant pose associated with the interaction, then we select the bounding box based on the joint configuration of the poselet to determine the best location to sample motion information from. After that we calculate the descriptors which, finally, are to be trained to acquire the detection model.

The first stage of the pipeline consists of locating the key joints of interest in the Kinect data. For a hand shake or a high five, these are the right shoulder, elbow, wrist and hand joints. For other interactions, other joints may be used. Using these key joints, we determine suitable frames in the learning data to extract a poselet that is representative for the particular interaction. Such an anchor frame can be regarded as containing a key pose. We hand-pick a seed frame at the epitome of the interaction from a random video. Next, we find in all other training sequences the most similar frame in terms of the Procrustus distance between the joint configuration of this seed frame and all frames in the sequence, following [7]. We rank all these frames based on the residual error. The frames below a certain threshold are ignored. Typically, we use a value between 0.5 and 0.75 as the threshold, which keeps the variance in the limb configuration low, while still retaining a sufficient number of sequences to learn the poselet from. The results of the selection procedure can be seen in Figure 2.

Based on this selection procedure, we retain a set of sequences to sample the frames from to create poselets for each of the two people involved in the interaction. As we know the anchor frame in each of the videos, we take this frame as the epitome of the interaction from which we sample the HOG descriptor. We consider the relative size and aspect ratio of all bounding boxes around the limbs involved in the interaction. These points determine two bounding boxes, one for each person. We warp the bounding boxes into the shape of the seed bounding box. The joint information from the Kinect metadata is also warped accordingly.

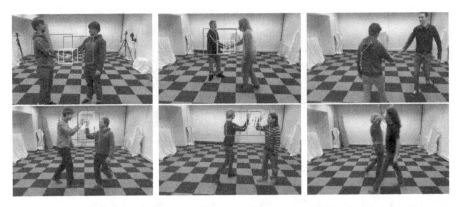

Fig. 2. Processed frames with respect to a seed frame (left): one with low (middle, both $RE = 0.15$) and one with high (right, $RE = 0.81$ and $RE = 0.52$) residual error. The bounding boxes are omitted in the rightmost images because they are not used for poselet creation, as the residual error exceeds the threshold.

Around these joints, we place a bounding box with a margin to the left top most joint (e.g., the right shoulder) and the right bottom most joint (e.g., the right hand). The margin size is chosen relative to the size of the skeleton in the seed frame.

After selecting suitable bounding boxes based on the joint locations provided by the metadata, we sample the HOG features for each of the two persons in the interaction. The size of the HOG template is determined by the size of the bounding box in the seed frame. The sizes of the two HOG templates are independent of each other. We use the HOG implementation described in [5] with both contrast insensitive (9 bins) and contrast sensitive features (18 bins), as well as 4 texture features. The resulting vector length is 31 data points per HOG cell.

While sampling the video data, we also track the relative positions of one person's limb with respect to the other's. This position allows us to calculate the mean offset of the limb bounding boxes. We process each of the sequences in our data in this manner. After extracting all the descriptors from the learning data, we determine the average offset of the two models with respect to each other. We also keep track of the relative positions of the joints within the poselet, to be able to sample the motion data from a specific position during the detection stage, without the need for additional pose information. The approach described here results in two poselets and their accompanying HOG representations. In Figure 3, we show the poselets for the hand shake interaction. These two HOG models are acquired by learning two separate linear Support Vector Machines (SVM), one for each class, that take the poselet vectors as positive data and randomly selected HOG vectors from the background images of the scene, as the negative learning data. Since we have a video stream from a static camera, it is easy to find frames that have little or no foreground information. Alternatively, random image data could be used. The models can also be trained using random

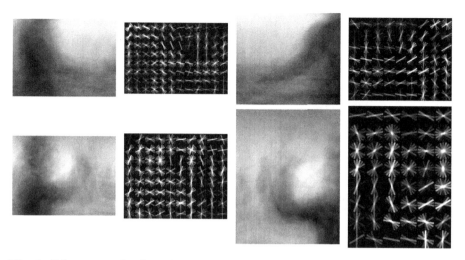

Fig. 3. Columns 1 and 3 show the normalized summed pixel values within the bounding boxes aligned by the anchor frame detection procedure, respectively for the right hand of the left and right person. Columns 2 and 3 show the corresponding HOG descriptors. Top row depicts the hand shake, the bottom a high five interaction. Note that the variance in the high five interaction is larger than in the hand shake interaction. This is due to the fact that the high five interaction is performed quicker, and has more variation in hand movement.

images that do not contain any humans, but we found that using the scenes background as negative learning data improves performance of the model. This is comparable to performing background subtraction.

Using the poselets, we can identify key poses of each of the two persons in the dyad. Since we are concerned with detecting fine-grained actions rather than just key poses, we enhance the HOG model with detailed movement information defined by a HOF descriptor. Adding motion information allows the detector to reject sequences where the poses match the model, though the motion information indicates otherwise. For instance, we can imagine two people standing hand-in-hand, being nearly indistinguishable from a hand shake by pose alone. We can find precise movement information within the poselet by taking advantage of the joint information provided by the Kinect. However, we want to create a model that will not depend on the Kinect data in the testing phase. This will increase the application potential of the method as video sequences are more commonly available. With the Kinect data in the training phase, not only can we speed up the selection of relevant frames, we can also learn a model that measures the movement of the actor only where it matters most: at the joint locations. It was shown in [11] that using the precise joint locations for movement measurements will give the best cues for action recognition. By defining a bounding box around the measured Kinect joint locations, we can enhance the HOG shape model with HOF movement descriptors, from which we classify the interaction more precisely.

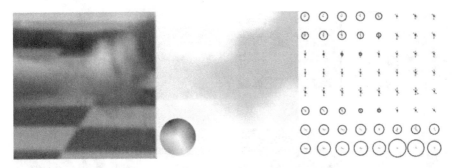

Fig. 4. Input image (left) with optical flow (middle) and visualization of the resulting HOF descriptor (right). The HOF visualization depicts directional arrows and circles. The length and direction of the arrows are indicative of the averaged magnitude and directional bin of the flow field histogram. The circles are indicative of the 0-bin of the histogram for parts of the flow field where no movement is present.

To build the HOF descriptors, we use an optical flow measurement inside a bounding box around the joints of the poselet. We create a HOF descriptor from the DeepFlow optical flow vectors [19] in the τ frames around the anchor frame. This sequence covers the movement at the joint location in such a way that a HOF descriptor with stable uniform movement directions can be created, as can be seen in Figure 4. The bounding box size is based on a square box on the seed frame. However, for the other sequences the bounding box may be warped by the same amount that the limb bounding box was warped due to the distortion of the limb, compared to the limb configuration in the seed frame. For the margin around the joint of interest on the seed frame we chose 32 pixels. The 15 joint motion sequence frames are clustered into 3×5 frames in which the movement directions are averaged for each of the 3 clusters. In each we create a directional grid much like the HOF descriptor described in [3]. However, a significant difference is that we use a regular grid instead of a flowing grid of keypoints, because we want our descriptor to be equally long for every measurement, as we do not use a bag-of-words approach for our classifier. The rightmost image of Figure 4 shows a visualization of our HOF output. Eventually, our detection model consists of a concatenation of this HOF descriptor to the HOG vector that describes the specific arm pose. The concatenated vector is learned by the soft margin linear SVM.

A separate SVM is trained for each of the two action classes. For negative learning data we use the scene's background for the static HOG part of the descriptor. For the HOF part of the negative feature descriptor we concatenate random movement samples from the dataset presented in [15].

3.2 Detecting and Classifying Interactions from Video Sequences

Given a sequence of frames, our method detects the occurence of a dyadic action in both time and space. For this, we use a sliding window approach. During testing, we use the two HOG/HOF models and the relative displacements of the

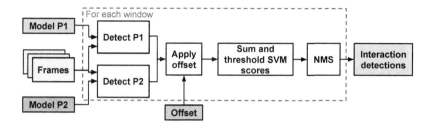

Fig. 5. Detection pipeline of the proposed approach. Refer to text for details.

models with respect to each other, see Figure 5. In the case of detecting hand shake and high five actions, we use the two models to detect the right arms of the two people involved in the interaction. We evaluate all possible locations of the poses and movements in a given frame. We apply the displacement offset and sum the results of the SVM scores on the detection results of the frame, shown in Figure 6. Then we use non-maximum suppression (NMS) to find the most likely position of the interaction of interest. The leftmost image in Figure 6 shows the detection of the right arm of the left person. There are false positive detections to the right of the right person. These scores are suppressed by adding the score of the right arm detection for the right person (second image). The sum detection result is shown in the third image. The fourth image shows the final detection after applying NMS. We show the ground truth location of the hand shake, determined by the Kinect, as a blue bounding box. The green bounding box is the top score that exceeds the threshold, the red bounding boxes are detections not exceeding the threshold.

Fig. 6. Normalized detection scores for two single person models (first and second image), the cumulative score (third image) and the final detection result (fourth image)

4   Experiments and Results

In this section, we give an overview of our experiments and results. We first introduce our novel ShakeFive dataset[1], followed by a discussion of the baseline method, against which we compare our dyadic interaction detection method.

---

[1] The dataset is publicly available for research purposes and can be downloaded from http://www.projects.science.uu.nl/shakefive/

4.1   ShakeFive Dataset

There is a number of datasets available that focus on detecting human interactions from video. A well known interaction dataset is the TV Human Interaction Dataset [18]. It contains 300 video clips containing several interactions (hug, hand shake, high five and kiss) from TV shows. The clips are unconstrained in terms of viewpoint, lighting and occlussions. They are often cut mid action, which our approach cannot handle. The UT-Interaction dataset [20] contains six classes of continuous interactions between two people in 20 different videos. The interactions are recorded from a static viewpoint but the classes contain movements that are performed with different parts of the body.

To be able to perform experiments in our targeted setting with a fixed camera viewpoint observing fine-grained interactions, we have chosen to record our own ShakeFive dataset of dyadic interactions. The dataset consists of 100 RGB videos, as well as Kinect skeleton measurements for each individual involved. Each video contains 2 people who perform one of two possible interactions: a hand shake or a high five.

There are 57 videos containing hand shake interactions and 43 containing high five interactions. They are performed by a total of 37 unique individuals, 35 males and 2 females. The RGB video resolution is 640x480 pixels, recorded at 15 frames per second, with an average length of about 145 frames. In Figure 7, we show two example frames from the dataset. The videos are accompanied by metadata files that contain frame numbers, 20 skeleton joint positions per person acquired by Kinect (if there is a person in the frame), and one of 5 possible labels describing the interaction in the frame: standing, approaching, hand shake, high five, leaving.

Fig. 7. Examples from ShakeFive dataset: hand shake (left) and high five (right)

4.2   Baseline

We compare our approach to the trajectory bag-of-words method of Wang *et al.* [3], which can be considered state-of-the-art. The method starts by finding trajectories of keypoints in an image sequence using a combination of HOG, HOF and Motion Boundary Histograms (MBH). Using these dense trajectories, a bag-of-visual-words (BoVW) codebook with 4,000 clusters is created using k-means. As the dense trajectories are already normalized, we do not normalize any further during this step. Following [3], we then create the codebook from the best of 8 k-means clusterings, found by sampling 100,000 randomly chosen data points from the complete descriptor set. After creating the BoVW codebook, we use it to create a codeword for every 5 annotated frames in the training videos. Using these codewords, a binary classifier is learned using a Support Vector Machine. We use a Histogram Intersection Kernel, which has been shown to give superior results [21]. We normalize the codeword histograms using the L1-norm. During testing we generate an L1-normalized histogram codeword for the given frame, which is then fed to the classification model, leading to a binary classification which indicates whether or not the frame contains the interaction of interest.

In its original formulation, the baseline approach takes into account the entire image frame. Motion due to the camera or due to objects and other people in the foreground and background can affect the extracted trajectories in both the training and test sets. To make a closer comparison to our own implementation, we also run the baseline method using a sliding window approach in combination with NMS. We use the same codebook but take the average interaction window size to extract the keypoints to create the codeword at the particular sub-frame within the current frame. We train a new model on this input. During testing, we slide the window over the frame and classify every sub-frame, followed by NMS to obtain the final candidates, similar to the proposed method.

4.3   Results

The performance of the model is measured using a 4-fold cross validation, in which for the hand shake classification we use 42 randomly chosen video sequences, together with the additional hand picked seed frame video, making a total of 43 training videos containing a hand shake. We use the other 14 videos to test the model we train. The high five interaction is trained using 30 videos plus the seed video and is tested on the remaining 12 videos. For the sliding window approaches, both in the dyadic interaction detection and the baseline approach, we use a stride of 16 pixels in both directions. During testing, a window is counted as correct when more than 50% of it overlaps with the ground truth window in that frame.

We show the results of our experiments on the ShakeFive dataset in Table 1. We measure the performance of the algorithms with the Mean Average Precision (MAP) of the four folds. During testing we ran the detector on every 10th frame of the video, from which we create short sequences of 15 frames ($\tau = 7$). This is approximately one second, and the value was empirically determined.

Our method scores an average precision of 49.56% using 75% of the available data for training and 25% for testing, using an exhaustive search with a sliding window on the tested frames. We have also tested the robustness of our method by reducing the amount of training data to 25%, while testing on the remaining three folds. This only slightly reduced the performance of the method both on

Table 1. MAP scores of the different methods on the ShakeFive dataset. For the proposed dyadic poselets method, we evaluated distributions of the training/test data of 75%/25% and 25%/75%.

Method	Hand shake	High five
Dyadic poselets (.75/.25)	**49.56**	**34.85**
Dyadic poselets (.25/.75)	47.87	23.94
Baseline	26.24	30.15
Baseline (sliding window)	20.10	23.07

the hand shake data and the high five data, showing its robustness. The hand shake data proves to be more robust than the high five data. Figure 8 makes the difference between the two types of interactions and the amounts of learning data clear. We can explain this by the speed of the interaction. A high five is a quick interaction compared to a hand shake. The sum images in Figure 3 show that the variation in the learning data is larger for the high five than it is for the hand shake. We can explain this by taking into account that the speed of the interaction in combination with the frame rate cause the matching of the poselets to be more difficult. This, in turn, makes the model less reliable, causing the larger drop in performance.

The baseline dense trajectory model gives an overall MAP performance for the implicit method for the hand shake action of 26.24% using the whole frame for classification and 20.10% for the sliding window approach. Here, the high five model performs slightly better (about 3-4%) than the hand shake model. We believe this is due to the fact that the dense trajectories on which the model is based are better capable of handling the fast motion of the high five. The performance of the baseline method stays below our method in both cases though. We believe this is because our model captures the pose and motion of the relevant body part for the given interaction more directly.

The sliding window approach on the baseline method slightly degrades performance on the baseline method. We believe this is due to the difference in the amount of classification windows. While the whole frame BoVW classifies a single interction per frame, using a sliding window approach in this case causes the system to classify more windows per frame. As a result the amount of false positives slightly increase because in considering more sub windows per frame, that do not contain the target action, the chance of a false detection increases.

Currently our method tries to find the frames that have limb configurations most similar to the limbs in the seed frame. This is not ideal. One of the issues here is that there are different view points of the interaction in the data, that will be missed by a model that is trained from one particular angle, which is bad for recall. Another issue is with the pose and motion slightly before and after the interaction. In the ground truth we chose to annotate the frame labels with some margin, so a hand shake for instance is already labeled as such when the person is moving his hand towards the hand of the other person. As we model the handshake at the epitome of the interaction, the frames where the hands are not yet joined together will not be detected and marked as false negative. A temporal structure as proposed in [10] could be employed to solve this problem. Finally, we notice an issue with the placement of the joint locations over time. The update speed of the Kinect joints seems to be insufficient to follow the precise hand location during the interaction, causing the ground truth locations to be inaccurate at certain frames. While the Kinect does a good job at giving the vicinity of the limbs, we find that the final position of the end of the limbs, such as the feet or hands, is often inaccurate. In training, this in turn causes the location of where the motion is sampled from, for a given example with respect to the limb templatate in the frame, to be less than optimal.

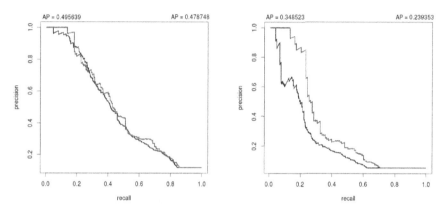

Fig. 8. The precision-recall diagrams for hand shake (left; red line, 0.75/0.25: $AP = 0.50$; blue line, 0.25/0.75: $AP = 0.48$) and high five (right; red line, 0.75/0.25: $AP = 0.35$; blue line, 0.25/0.75: $AP = 0.24$)

5   Conclusion and Future Work

We have presented an approach to detect, in space and time, fine-grained dyadic interactions from videos. We rely on a combination of pose and flow information to detect typical body poses of each person and the coordination of their joint movement, respectively. During training, we use joint pose information obtained using Kinect to speed up the selection of relevant frames to train the detectors. We have introduced the novel ShakeFive dataset that contains two-person hand shake and high five interactions to evaluate our method. In our experiments, our dyadic interaction detection method outperforms the baseline approach of Wang et al. [3]. Reducing the amount of training to 10-14 sequences only slightly reduces the performance in terms of average precision.

The motion information in the data provides us with good cues for enhancing the pose related to the coordinated interaction. We show how to add this motion information to a structured model that relies on poselets for interaction detection. The ShakeFive dataset contains the pose information that can be used as a stepping stone for learning dyadic interactions. This is helpful in providing a simple way to get ground-truth information for the people involved in the interaction.

We identify several potential avenues for improvement of our approach. At this moment, we rely on a restricted viewpoint under which the the interaction is observed. During training, we ignore examples where the limbs of the people are too different from those in the seed frame. We would like to include these examples to achieve view invariancy to a certain extend. We can solve this by introducing multiple components, which model different angles separately, as in [5].

Currently, the contribution to our model from both HOG and HOF are weighted equally. In future work we would like to enhance the model and weigh the contribution of HOG and HOF depending on the motion and shape of the interaction. We intend to use the work by Mittal *et al.* [22] to perform structured output SVM ranking on the trained linear SVM outputs of our model.

We believe the placement of the joint locations from which the HOF is sampled could be improved by treating them as latent variables in our model. That means that the joint location in a poselet from which the motion is sampled, is not exactly fixed. This location acts as an initial indication of where the motion should be sampled from in the frame, but is then updated in an iterative fashion as is done in [5] for the location of the object parts with respect to the root of the template in that frame.

Finally, we will investigate to what extent the proposed approach can be used to detect dyadic, coordinated social behavior in conversations. The encouraging results on hand shakes and high five interactions have demonstrated the ability to detect fine-grained coordinated interactions involving the hands. We are interested to see how the method performs on interactions that involve other body parts, such as is the case with hugging and kissing. Ultimately, we would like to detect a range of meaningful dyadic interactions to better understand social behavior.

References

1. Poppe, R.: A survey on vision-based human action recognition. Image and Vision Computing 28(6), 976–990 (2010)
2. Schuldt, C., Laptev, I., Caputo, B.: Recognizing human actions: A local SVM approach. In: Proceedings International Conference on Pattern Recognition (ICPR), Cambridge, UK, pp. 32–36 (2004)
3. Wang, H., Kläser, A., Schmid, C., Cheng-Lin, L.: Dense trajectories and motion boundary descriptors for action recognition. International Journal of Computer Vision (IJCV) 103(1), 60–79 (2013)
4. Felzenszwalb, P.F., Huttenlocher, D.: Pictorial structures for object recognition. International Journal of Computer Vision (IJCV) 61(1), 55–79 (2005)
5. Felzenszwalb, P.F., Girshick, R.B., McAllester, D.A., Ramanan, D.: Object detection with discriminatively trained part-based models. IEEE Transactions on Pattern Analysis and Machine Intelligence (PAMI) 32(9), 1627–1645 (2010)
6. Yang, Y., Ramanan, D.: Articulated human detection with flexible mixtures of parts. IEEE Transactions on Pattern Analysis and Machine Intelligence (PAMI) 35(12), 2878–2890 (2013)

7. Bourdev, L., Malik, J.: Poselets: Body part detectors trained using 3D human pose annotations. In: Proceedings IEEE International Conference on Computer Vision (ICCV), Kyoto, Japan, pp. 1365–1372 (2009)
8. Maji, S., Bourdev, L.D., Malik, J.: Action recognition from a distributed representation of pose and appearance. In: Proceedings IEEE Conference on Computer Vision and Pattern Recognition (CVPR). Colorado Springs, CO, pp. 3177–3184 (2011)
9. Raptis, M., Sigal, L.: Poselet key-framing: A model for human activity recognition. In: Proceedings IEEE Conference on Computer Vision and Pattern Recognition (CVPR), Portland, OR, pp. 2650–2657 (2013)
10. Yao, B.Z., Nie, B.X., Liu, Z., Zhu, S.C.: Animated pose templates for modeling and detecting human actions. IEEE Transactions on Pattern Analysis and Machine Intelligence (PAMI) 36(3), 436–452 (2014)
11. Jhuang, H., Gall, J., Zuffi, S., Schmid, C., Black, M.J.: Towards understanding action recognition. In: Proceedings IEEE International Conference on Computer Vision (ICCV), Sydney, Australia, pp. 3192–3199 (2013)
12. Gupta, A., Kembhavi, A., Davis, L.: Observing human-object interactions: Using spatial and functional compatibility for recognition. IEEE Transactions on Pattern Analysis and Machine Intelligence (PAMI) 31(10), 1775–1789 (2009)
13. Yao, B., Fei-Fei, L.: Recognizing human-object interactions in still images by modeling the mutual context of objects and human poses. IEEE Transactions on Pattern Analysis and Machine Intelligence (PAMI) 34(9), 1691–1703 (2012)
14. Lan, T., Wang, Y., Yang, W., Robinovitch, S.N., Mori, G.: Discriminative latent models for recognizing contextual group activities. IEEE Transactions on Pattern Analysis and Machine Intelligence 34(8), 1549–1562 (2012)
15. Choi, W., Savarese, S.: Understanding collective activities of people from videos. IEEE Transactions on Pattern Analysis and Machine Intelligence (PAMI) 36(6), 1242–1257 (2014)
16. Cristani, M., Bazzani, L., Paggetti, G., Fossati, A., Tosato, D., Del Bue, A., Menegaz, G., Murino, V.: Social interaction discovery by statistical analysis of F-formations. In: Proceedings British Machine Vision Conference (BMVC), Dundee, United Kingdom, pp. 1–12 (2011)
17. Chang, M.C., Krahnstoever, N., Ge, W.: Probabilistic group-level motion analysis and scenario recognition. In: Proceedings IEEE International Conference on Computer Vision (ICCV), Barcelona, Spain, pp. 747–754 (2011)
18. Patron-Perez, A., Marszałek, M., Reid, I., Zisserman, A.: Structured learning of human interactions in tv shows. IEEE Transactions on Pattern Analysis and Machine Intelligence (PAMI) 34(12), 2441–2453 (2012)
19. Weinzaepfel, P., Revaud, J., Harchaoui, Z., Schmid, C.: DeepFlow: Large displacement optical flow with deep matching. In: Proceedings IEEE International Conference on Computer Vision (ICCV), Sydney, Australia, pp. 1385–1392 (2013)
20. Ryoo, M.S., Aggarwal, J.K.: UT-Interaction Dataset, ICPR contest on semantic description of human activities, SDHA (2010),
http://cvrc.ece.utexas.edu/SDHA2010/Human_Interaction.html
21. Maji, S., Berg, A.C., Malik, J.: Classification using intersection kernel support vector machines is efficient. In: Proceedings IEEE Conference on Computer Vision and Pattern Recognition (CVPR), Anchorage, AK, pp. 1–8 (2008)
22. Mittal, A., Blaschko, M.B., Zisserman, A., Torr, P.H.S.: Taxonomic multi-class prediction and person layout using efficient structured ranking. In: Fitzgibbon, A., Lazebnik, S., Perona, P., Sato, Y., Schmid, C. (eds.) ECCV 2012, Part II. LNCS, vol. 7573, pp. 245–258. Springer, Heidelberg (2012)

Author Index